MW01089208

SPINOZA FOR OUR TIME

INSURRECTIONS: CRITICAL STUDIES IN
RELIGION, POLITICS, AND CULTURE

Insurrections: Critical Studies in Religion, Politics, and Culture

Slavoj Žižek, Clayton Crockett, Creston Davis, Jeffrey W. Robbins, Editors

The intersection of religion, politics, and culture is one of the most discussed areas in theory today. It also has the deepest and most wide-ranging impact on the world. Insurrections: Critical Studies in Religion, Politics, and Culture will bring the tools of philosophy and critical theory to the political implications of the religious turn. The series will address a range of religious traditions and political viewpoints in the United States, Europe, and other parts of the world. Without advocating any specific religious or theological stance, the series aims nonetheless to be faithful to the radical emancipatory potential of religion.

FOR THE LIST OF TITLES IN THIS SERIES, SEE PAGE 127

SPINOZA FOR OUR TIME
Politics and Postmodernity

Antonio Negri

Translated by William McCuaig

Columbia University Press

New York

COLUMBIA UNIVERSITY PRESS

Publishers Since 1893

New York   Chichester, West Sussex

cup.columbia.edu

Spinoza et nous d'Antonio Negri © 2010 Editions Galilée

English translation copyright © 2013 Columbia University Press

Library of Congress Cataloging-in-Publication Data

Negri, Antonio, 1933–

  [Spinoza et nous. English]

  Spinoza for our time : politics and postmodernity / Antonio Negri ;
translated by William McCuaig.

     pages cm

  Includes bibliographical references and index.

  ISBN 978-0-231-16046-9 (cloth : alk. paper) —
ISBN 978-0-231-50066-1 (e-book)

  1. Spinoza, Benedictus de, 1632–1677.   I. Title.

B3998.N4413   2013

199'.492—dc23   2012051155

Columbia University Press books are printed on permanent
and durable acid-free paper.

This book is printed on paper with recycled content.

Printed in the United States of America

c 10 9 8 7 6 5 4 3 2 1

Cover design by Martin Hinze

CONTENTS

FOREWORD

Time is restless.

—ANTONIO NEGRI, *Time for Revolution*, "kairòs"

Our relation to the seventeenth-century Dutch Jewish philosopher Baruch Spinoza via the twenty-first century Italian thinker Antonio Negri is to an unthought or barely thought radical democracy, a concrete potentiality and smoldering power of our time. In the *Ethics*, Spinoza provides us with an ontology and an anthropology of creative relations, a constructive account of immanent being on the one hand and, on the other, an affective, desiring conception of human liberation achieved through embodied joy and intellectual power. In his other great work, the *Theological-Political Treatise*, Spinoza leads us—against the mainstream modern political tradition and, today, against neoliberalism—to a concept of democracy understood as "a society which wields all its power as a whole" (ch. XVI, Elwes translation). Negri's decades-long work on Spinoza aims to demonstrate both how these two sides of Spinoza's vision cohere and how they mutually reinforce one another. For Negri, the genius of Spinoza was to have grasped at the epochal inception of modernity, among the forces of its incipient capitalist globalization, the ultimate identity of an immanent, material, affective, and constructive conception of being and a unique idea of democratic political constitution.

For Negri, the word "democracy," far from merely signifying one political system among others, one, say, in which individuals would be allowed the freedom to choose their governmental representatives and to engage freely in exchange-relations with others, designates instead an ontologically creative power, *the* universal human power—political, but equally social, cultural, linguistic, physical—to make and remake being itself. A cooperation-without-synthesis of subjective and material forces acting in common, such democracy manifests the irreversible power to make the world itself a common space of creative endeavor, thereby forging new relations that amplify unlimitedly that very power itself. This form of action inhabits a unique temporality, the time of *kairòs*—the creative moment that ruptures the continuous flow of ordinary history and opens up not only new possibilities and new names but new realities. There is nothing abstract about this common power, *our* common power. It is the concrete, global interconnectedness of human labor and life, born in principle with the advent of modernity and yet immediately curtailed and distorted by the brutal history of modern capitalism. Among other things, democracy is a name—sullied, to be sure, but infinitely self-renewing—for action oriented not toward but within the affects of joy and love (*real* joy and *real* love, not the cheap substitutes proffered and withdrawn everywhere in the service of other ends). Democracy asserts the immanence of this world's desiring multitude.

In developing such a concept of radical democracy across the dozens of books he has written over the past decades, Negri conjoins politics and ontology in a program of the noncapitalist production of a global common. And in this conjunction Spinoza remains for Negri the key thinker. Where Spinoza wrote *Deus, sive Natura*—*God, or Nature*—to mark the unqualified identification of two terms designating concepts usually held not only to be distinct but to be positively opposed to one another, Negri offers us a similarly momentous fusion of concepts, at once philosophical and political: *democracy, or communism*. For Negri, such a fusion does not represent some exterior synthesis or merely ideal approximation, but is rather the immanent naming of the constitutive and joyful power that Spinoza was the first to identify philosophically as the very substance of our world. This is indeed *our* ontology, the ontology of the multitude, a theory and praxis fusing objective and subjective genitives in a new political grammar.

The present work, *Spinoza for Our Time*, has roots in some of Negri's earliest projects. Already in books such as *Political Descartes* and, later, *Marx Beyond Marx*, Negri employs philosophy's embeddedness in large-scale social and historical processes as a way to advance a style of textual analysis and rigorous argumentation that takes the dynamics of such processes into account in the reading of the history of philosophy without reductionism or vicious circularity. In Negri's work an immanently political writing is thereby made manifest, a powerful inscription of historical materials and theory into channels of immediate political resonance. Like Machiavelli before him, Negri writes equally in the immediate political present and in the attenuated presence of his historical interlocutors. And like Machiavelli, Negri knows the fierce immediacy of political struggle and the ineliminable need for the sharpest intellectual cunning, not to mention the negativity and brutality of reactionary power, of the forces of punishment and imprisonment that aim to crush bodies and minds that will not submit. In Negri's writing, thought bodies forth the materiality of a rhythmic, driving assault. The clarity of his arguments and the detail of his textual examinations as well as the force and frequent brilliance of his rhetorical leaps at once exhibit and produce a distinctive intellectual camaraderie. One reads *with* him, and one is invited by the force of the argument and its narrativization to add one's own powers of thought to its uncompromising movement. In Negri's writing, thought itself learns the impulse of its essentially political drive.

Negri's militancy is everywhere steeped in a deep erudition that draws upon multiple sources, including the Italian humanist tradition, the metaphysics and political thought of modern philosophy, and the most sophisticated theoretical developments of late modernity and postmodernity. It is important to keep in mind, however, that the roots of his rhetorical and argumentative power are to be found above all in the concrete political struggles Negri has waged and continues to wage on solitary and collective fronts. His work with the Autonomia movement in Italy in the 1970s and his direct engagement with workers' revolts and factory occupations during that time imbue his thinking with a firsthand understanding of the dynamics of collective resistance, a veritable physics and chemistry of revolutionary action. The tactics and strategy of Autonomia were in many ways opposed to those of the dominant leftist organization in Italy at the time, the Italian Communist Party (PCI), and this antagonistic difference internal to the left becomes for Negri one microcosm or synecdoche of a more general struggle of creative freedom against command, of immanence against transcendence, and of true communism against the Party and the State. In this way, Negri was able to bring the theoretical advances of the French philosophers of the 1960s and 1970s (in particular, Foucault, Deleuze, and Guattari) to bear on the concrete political concerns of his day, asserting a method of molecular resonance as against that of synthetic molarity. A new image of revolutionary praxis thus emerged, a seemingly paradoxical conjunction, as Negri put it at the time, of Rosa Luxemburg and Vladimir Lenin, an anarchist-collectivist broadbased vanguard. This distinctive viewpoint continues to inform Negri's more recent solo writings and collaborations, and both of these have been subject to a good deal of criticism from left and right. It may be noted here in passing that seldom have the critics of the concepts of Empire and Multitude that grew out of this early work been themselves able to speak from such a first-person standpoint conjoining the most rigorous academic research with the experience of direct struggle, high-level academic production with effective factory takeover.

In the wake of the kidnapping and assassination of the Italian Christian-Democratic politician Aldo Moro by the radical leftist Red Brigades in 1978, Negri was accused under highly dubious pretenses of instigating terrorism and being involved with the murder. Although he was absolved of those charges, he was eventually convicted on separate, also quite dubious counts. He would later flee to France and receive political asylum there. While in Italian prison, however, awaiting his trial, Negri wrote *The Savage Anomaly: The Power of Spinoza's Metaphysics and Politics*, one of the finest works on Spinoza written in the twentieth century and a pivotal text in the renaissance of Spinoza scholarship that flourished in the 1960s with works by such thinkers as Matheron, Moreau, Althusser, Balibar, Macherey, and Deleuze and that continues today through the work of Zourabichvili, Vinciguerra, Montag, Tosel, Kordela, Israel, and many others. The core argument of *The Savage Anomaly* depends upon a sustained analysis of the difference between two concepts of power in the *Ethics*: on the one hand, *potestas*, a capacity to act and create effects, a broadly "dialectical" power—linked definitively to transcendence—corresponding somewhat to Aristotelian *dynamis*, that is, a power that subsists as *possibility* and gathers itself essentially in its inhibition and in its self-restraint; on the other hand, *potentia*, the exercise of force *in situ* and *in actu*, the constitutive activity that coordinates subjective desire and objective construction in a genuinely immanent creation. This distinction of *potestas* and *potentia* serves as the basis for a coordination of the themes and arguments of Spinoza's *Ethics* and his *Theological-Political Treatise* in terms of a "phenomenology of revolutionary praxis constitutive of the future." Negri takes the break in the composition of the *Ethics* in which Spinoza writes and publishes the *Theological-Political Treatise* as more than an accidental biographical detail, as instead the necessary passage in the construction of the ontology of the *Ethics* through the immediate political crisis that marks the composition of the *Treatise*. Spinoza and Negri's phenomenology of praxis thus becomes one of an immediate situating of thought within the crisis of capitalism. Only the clear-sighted confrontation with the contemporary political and economic crisis enables Spinoza's ontology to mark the thoroughgoing immanentization of thought, which Negri interprets, controversially, as an inversion of the relationship between the unity of substance and the plurality of its modes. For Negri, a privileging of the constitutive relationality of the modes over and against the unity of substance becomes the measure of a final shift in Spinoza's thought away from the residual transcendence still evident in the earlier work of the *Short Treatise* and the *Emendation of the Intellect*. With this constitutive modal turn, this *political* turn, in the composition history of Spinoza's *Ethics*, Negri thus identifies the very moment at which an irreversible ontological event inaugurates within philosophy the immanent singularity of a global common.

In 1997 Negri returned to Italy voluntarily from his political asylum in France to serve out the remainder of his sentence. He remained mostly under house arrest until 2003, when he became, after decades of imprisonment, exile, and then highly restricted mobility, at last relatively free to travel, meet with others, and speak publicly and in person at academic and political venues. This period from 1997 to the present has seen the publication of the three installments of Negri's collaboration with Michael Hardt—*Empire*, *Multitude*, and *Commonwealth*—which have made Negri's work more widely known and discussed, and a number of other texts by him have appeared. Not surprisingly, among the many talks he has given during this period, he has returned frequently to Spinoza as to a comrade who has supported him in the past and continues to reside with him in the present.

Spinoza for Our Time collects four talks given by Negri on Spinoza at various colloquia and conferences between 2005 and 2009. This collection both continues and supplements the essays gathered in Negri's *The Subversive Spinoza*, published in 1992, which addressed, among other themes, the status of Spinoza's unfinished *Political Treatise*, the subterranean connections between Spinozan thought and the poetics of Leopardi, and the key contrast of philosophical approaches indexed by the names Spinoza and Heidegger. The texts of the four presentations in *Spinoza for Our Time* are preceded by Negri's extended introduction, which accomplishes several tasks concurrently: revisiting the main theses of *The Savage Anomaly*; reviewing the major figures in Continental Spinoza studies over the past several decades; and situating his ongoing philosophical project within the broader contemporary scene of Continental political philosophy. Regarding this last point, Alain Badiou, Emanuele Severino, and the Schmitt-influenced political theologies of Derrida and Agamben are directly confronted in striking contrast with Negri's own project and in particular his well-known collaborations with Hardt. The basic orientation of *The Savage Anomaly* is strongly reasserted as against these current philosophical trends, and in this way *Spinoza for Our Time* is intended both to clarify and to focus the perhaps better-known analyses of *Empire, Multitude,* and *Commonwealth.* The introduction is thus in part intended to demonstrate the continuity of the philosophical-political project that has carried Negri from his earliest writings and political activities through to the contemporary conjuncture.

The four essays that then follow, taken together, present the outline of a coherent intervention and reassertion of Spinoza's relevance to the contemporary debates outlined in the introduction. The first essay, "Spinoza: A Heresy of Immanence and of Democracy," revisits the primary philosophical-historical thesis of *The Savage Anomaly* and works to show the relevance of the anomalous event of Spinoza's thought in early modern philosophy to contemporary global politics. Negri does not shy away here from asserting a sharp dichotomy, which is not to say that his analysis is at all unnuanced or brutal. In the juxtaposition of Bodin and Hobbes on the one hand with Spinoza on the other, we see the clear break that separates a political vision grounded in transcendence from one operating within immanence. Negri shows how this difference at its heart concerns the key Marxist distinction between the social relations of production and the forces of production themselves, the former transfigured by ideology, the latter inalienable in principle. Negri demonstrates the belonging of the mainstream social contract tradition to an ideological and reactionary inhibition of production by way of its necessary detour through transcendence. In opposition to this—but it is a thoroughly asymmetrical and nondialectical opposition—Spinoza's ethical ontology (being *is* praxis) makes the cooperation and collision of forces the very substance of social order and thus traces *in its own actuality and effectivity* the political object it engages. The common replaces the public through its essentially creative and productive excess with respect to every constituted order.

Somewhat more polemical with respect to contemporary philosophical trends is the second text, "Potency and Ontology: Heidegger or Spinoza." Negri's title plays on that of Pierre Macherey's seminal study *Hegel or Spinoza*, demonstrating in a somewhat different way the singularity of Spinoza's project of immanence, which forcefully opposes itself to every reaffirmation of transcendence, especially in the sophisticated forms marked by philosophers such as Hegel and Heidegger. Here, Negri attacks the Heideggerian interpretations of existential and post-*Kehre* temporality and argues that the supposed Heideggerian break with modern metaphysical conceptions of temporality is in fact far less radical than that of the apparently "eternalist" Spinoza, for whom *time* on Negri's provocative reading emerges as a constituent "time of power" productive of new being (as opposed to Heidegger's nihilistic "powerlessness of time"). Despite Heidegger's break with the Idealist tradition and its culmination in Hegel as well his own partial self-overcoming in the "Turning," Heidegger according to Negri remains essentially bound to the dissociation of actuality and affirmation that characterizes modernity. The contrast here is never crude, but it is definitive and clear. Both Heidegger and Spinoza mark a "return to earth," a human belonging to Being, but in the case of Heidegger this belonging can only be decided and affirmed as a giving-up or giving-over to the unthought event. With Spinoza, however, the cooperative experience of human world-creation appears as "a dimension both unremarkable and strong," in other words as the *common* that is at once the ground and the creative object of democratic action.

The crucial figure of Nietzsche links the contrast of Spinoza and Heidegger to the themes of the third essay, "Multitude and Singularity in the Development of Spinoza's Political Thought." This essay—developed from a talk given at the Jerusalem Spinoza Institute—insists upon the ontological basis of Spinoza's radical democracy in an immanent monism, as distinct from any theologically oriented reinsertion of transcendence as an external guarantee of democratic political forms. Taking as his point of departure the instances in Nietzsche's texts where Spinoza is represented in negative terms as an idealist and denier of vital affirmation, Negri aims to reconstitute the genealogy of productive social desire in the *Ethics*. Negri here emphasizes the moment of "mutation" that characterizes the desire connecting singularities, the emergence of productive relationality *between and across* singularities as they act in common, this praxis itself performing in a strictly immanent fashion the connective role later thinkers such as Hegel will relegate to the field of "mediation." This moment of mutation is essential for Negri, and helps to explain how Spinoza's ontology may retain the rigor of its "rationalism" while supporting a materially creative and truly vital productivity. Thus the *political essence* of human striving becomes manifest, an immanent (super)naturalism: "not the reconstruction of the organic but the construction of the common."

Finally, "Spinoza: A Sociology of the Affects" draws upon the key Spinozan concepts of *conatus, cupiditas,* and *amor* in conjunction with a turn to Foucauldian genealogy to oppose a constitutive Spinozan conception of the social to every abstract and individualist model—such as that, in particular, of the dominant modern natural-right tradition—in which concrete social relations supervene upon first-order independent actors and institutions. Once again, the refrain is sounded of an opposition of transcendence and immanence, in this case a contrast between static, atemporal models of sociality and intrinsically antagonistic, temporalized discourses of social transformation. Here, this distinction operates such that "we can descry in Spinoza . . . a perspective on actuality and an initiation into the desire to gain cognizance of the structures of society and power that are evolving right now." Importantly, Negri points to a variety of theorists in this context—Simmel, Becker, Bourdieu, Simondon, Althusser, Macherey, Foucault—who have already in one way or another made such an immanent terrain of social analysis their own. Each of these references indicates a path to follow, a channel for further research and creative, practical deployment.

The critical and affirmative force of Negri's thought is evident on every page. His canonical strategy is simple—and infectious: identify some form of thought inhibiting constructive and revolutionary political theory and praxis, and dismantle its theoretical presuppositions by way of Spinoza's positive and constitutive ontology. This strategy is at once historical, ontological, and political. Throughout these essays it is the coordination of three axes of interpretation that underlies Negri's view of Spinoza: an attention to the social and political context of early modern Europe, within which Spinoza worked; a profound immersion in the complexities, singularities, and overall topography of Spinoza's texts; and an unflagging sense of urgency via sustained reference to present and future political postmodernity.

The "we" invoked by the title *Spinoza for Our Time* is neither a generalized collective nor a narrow scholarly circle but instead a singular cross-section of a new kind of cooperative social and political subject defined primarily by its immanent forces of creative resistance rather than its composition through distinctive identities. It is perhaps Negri more than any other living intellectual who has best charted both the constitutive dynamics and the affirmative prognosis of such a subject. On the one hand, the relative informality of these texts (in comparison, for instance, with *The Savage Anomaly*) makes this collection a fine introduction to Negri's quite unique reading and application of Spinoza's metaphysics. Yet on the other hand the arguments laid out here also speak incisively to the growing community of advanced Spinoza scholarship that treats Spinoza's thought *in and of the present*, a scholarly community for whom the stakes of Spinoza's philosophy are also the stakes of the contemporary global political conjuncture.

This is thinking of and for our time. In the wake of the global economic crisis in 2008, radical political thought is undoubtedly in the midst of a resurgence in Europe, the United States, and throughout the world. Today, when "austerity" has become a faith-cry of increasing desperation beyond any principle of reason in the face of neoliberal default, it is time for renewed attention to the original bourgeois capitalist fracture that was opened in the age of Spinoza as well as to the heretical path charted by Spinoza's thought in response to this fractured opening, a response pregnant with futures largely obscured and postponed by the dominant traditions of metaphysics and ontology on the one hand and political philosophy on the other. Today Spinoza's—and Negri's—political and ontological conception gives impetus to our present all-too-necessary dismantling of the current order and—in the face of an undeniable reactive consolidation of economic and political *potestas*—the conjugation, at local and planetary levels, of noncapitalist modes of survival with strategies for the revolutionary construction of postcapitalist society.

Rocco Gangle
Endicott College

TRANSLATOR'S NOTE

The translation is based on the text published in French, *Spinoza et nous*. Although Judith Revel is credited as the translator of this book from the original Italian, and discusses the nuances of her Italian-to-French translation in several footnotes (which I omit here), her French text is considered definitive by the author. All that appears within square brackets is a gloss by me; all that appears within round brackets is a parenthetical remark by the author.

Antonio Negri quotes Spinoza's *Ethics* (in Latin, *Ethica*) frequently, the *Tractatus politicus* a handful of times, and the *Tractatus theologico-politicus* just once, all from published French translations. The English translation in the public domain of Spinoza's major works is by R. H. M. Elwes, and dates from the late nineteenth century. All the Elwes translations of Spinoza's works are available at the website of the Online Library of Liberty, a project of Liberty Fund; and his translation of the *Ethics* is also available at a valuable website hosted by Middle Tennessee State University, with hypertext coding of Spinoza's own complicated system of bracketed internal cross-references. These cross-references do not appear here because Antonio Negri follows the convention of silently omitting them from quoted passages.

I use the Elwes translation of Spinoza's *Ethics*, but I have occasionally seen fit to modify it slightly after comparing it to the Latin original. The Latin is easy to find online, but the edition I use is Spinoza, *Opera/Werke*, ed. and trans. Konrad Blumenstock, vol. 2 (Darmstadt: Wissenschaftliche Buchgesellschaft, 1967).

SPINOZA FOR OUR TIME

INTRODUCTION

Spinoza and Us

1. IN DEFENSE OF *THE SAVAGE ANOMALY*

Thirty years have now gone by since the publication of *The Savage Anomaly*.[1] I wrote it in prison, and when they ask me today how I managed that, I am sorry to have to say that the answer is still the same: resistance. Call it an instantiation of *potentia* if you like. Nor does my astonishment lessen as I leaf through *The Savage Anomaly* today, for not only does it remain relevant and hold its place in the scholarly literature on Spinoza, but even those critics (I marvel to note) who did react negatively to some of my positions or lines of interpretation were able to do so while remaining fully conscious that the reading in question—the interpretation of

Spinoza I was proposing—had irresistible force: it is Spinoza who grasped the energy that constructs modal singularities in absolute being; it is Spinoza who perceived, in the manner in which these come together with one another, the ontological unfolding of forms of life and institutions; it is Spinoza for whom notions held in common are simply deployed rationality.

Of course there have also been comments from people prepared to treat any reading of Spinoza grounded in the overarching continuity of *potentia* (in its ascent from the materiality of *conatus* to the corporality of *cupiditas* and on to the intelligence of *amor*) as no more than a sort of spiritual business venture—as though one were a peddler of false hope and illusionary comfort to people grappling with the tough job of living.[2] The reactionary rage of others is palpable as they try to deny that Spinoza attributed to the *democratia omnino absoluta* of the multitude the political role he did attribute to it.[3] Finally, I have been accused of exaggerating the opposition between *potentia* [potency, *puissance*] and *potestas* [power, *pouvoir*], and this opposition (which is in reality more interactive than oppositional) is supposed to have lured me into a species of Manichaeanism.[4] I must say, I do not think that my critics have landed any really telling blows.

The reason—I think it must now be acknowledged—that *The Savage Anomaly* was able to impose a new perspective on the interpretation of Spinoza was that it was part of a wider process of renewal of the traditions of thought about transformation. In other words it was swept up in the *epistémè* of innovation and revolution dating roughly from 1968 that rebuilt the foundations of the science of mind, in the wake of the brilliant highs and dark lows of "real socialism." But the main reason for the success of *The Savage Anomaly* must be that the perspective on Spinoza defended there revives the possibility of willing and acting consciously to transform or overthrow the capitalist mode of production, of asserting human equality and the human common.

Far from being isolated, I was just one of many who were working at the time on constructing the *epistémè* of a communism for tomorrow. Nor was I alone in working on Spinoza: let me mention the revered names of Alexandre Matheron[5] and Gilles Deleuze,[6] who also labored at a reconstruction of human history, from the depths of the *cupiditates* up to the summit of renewal and democracy. They in turn had been preceded by certain phenomenological and structuralist schools that had already grappled, post-1945, with the interconnection between the great theoretical and practical contradictions and the contemporary struggles by workers in Europe and throughout the advanced capitalist world to achieve absolute democracy.

Spinoza and 1968. The reinterpretation of Spinoza amid and after 1968. There you have a couple of fetching subtitles, a charming topos for the history of philosophy. It might not do for the sort of historiography whose functional purpose is to neutralize the living body of philosophy, and those of philosophers, to confine them once and for all in the realm of transcendental spirit, but it would do for philosophy that, through the critical adventure of reason and the experience of the multitudes, is there to pragmatically help us advance toward the realization of liberty.

Today we are living a new epoch. After the fall of "real socialism," capitalism tried to give itself a new aspect: the hegemony of cognitive labor, the expanding dimension of finance, the theme of imperial extension. Every one of these transmutations of capital is in crisis. Capitalism and its civilization have failed. Through new wars and new devastation, neoliberalism and its elites have brought the world to ruin. If he were alive, Baruch Spinoza would call them *ultimi barbarorum*. We have a real paradox here: Spinoza's tools for thinking, which seemed "abnormal" at the start of the modern era, have today become—at the boundary of modernity, on the edge of a "post-" that has turned contemporary—radically "alternative," *concretely* revolutionary. In the seventeenth century, when the critical and constructive experience of Spinozan thought sat alone in one pan of the balance, with all the weight of counter-reformation religiosity and the rise of absolute sovereignty on the other, it was branded as "savage." Today the word has a different ring, evoking multiple experiences of subversion and the arousal of the living potency of the multitudes.

When I reread it, I am no longer surprised by *The Savage Anomaly*: because this book is pregnant with self-realizing desire; because it is a dispositif captured in the act of constituting itself. As Deleuze put it so well,[7] it may be that once the infinite has been ripped free of all its divinized trappings, it is realized in us, in the coincidence of desire and reality. But that, in Spinoza, is also the common name of revolution.[8]

2. EXTENDING *THE ANOMALY* INTO POSTMODERNITY

Spinoza and us, then. Two critical moments in particular demand to be reckoned with. The first receives its reckoning in sections 3 and 4 of this introduction, which seek to outline what might be called a postmodern usage of Spinoza, following his trajectory from "abnormal" philosopher of modernity in the seventeenth century to "alternative" philosopher of the twenty-first-century crisis. In this perspective, it is essential to focus on the concept of potency and to perceive the production of subjectivity at the heart of Spinozan ontology. The objections advanced by those with an opposing research program boil down to promoting individualism as a primary theme in Spinozan philosophy—but if it were, Spinoza's ontology and political philosophy would not be any different from all the other schemes for social, political, and economic organization proposed and imposed by seventeenth-century thinkers.

Chapter 2 (which is discussed in greater detail in sections 5 and 6 of this introduction) attempts a fresh definition of Spinoza as the subversive philosopher who, from the seventeenth century through to the twenty-first, maintains ever more effectually the opposition between the positivity of being on one hand and the metaphysical or transcendental reduction of ontology on the other. There is no better way to show what postmodernity owes to Spinoza. Political society (in both its political and its economic dimensions) is a product of desire: there you have the truly subversive process. In Spinoza we have the creative reprise of Machiavelli's realism, just as, much later, we will witness, with Gramsci and with heterodox and libertarian Marxism, the creative reprise of Spinozism.

At the opposite extreme, there is man imprisoned by negative ontology. We still have this image and these metaphysical functionalities inside our heads, just as we have since antiquity, when the word *archè* designated both "principle" and "command." In the twentieth century, Heidegger was the most acute and compelling figure of this negative thought, and he left a mark that has not been effaced. An enemy of socialism, he pretends to accept its critique of the capitalist and technological world of reification and alienation, only to switch the polarity and claim that existence entails abandonment to the purity and the nakedness of being. But being and substance are never either pure or naked: they are always made of institutions and history, and the truth issues from struggle, and from the human construction of temporality itself.

If there exists a tragedy of the present labeled "alienation" or "reification," it is not determined by the being-for-death of human existence, but by the producing-for-death of capitalist power. Reactionary thought reconstructed itself around Heidegger and it reproduces itself in the ontology of nihilism. Subversive thought reconstructs itself around Spinozan ethics and politics and ontology. It is Spinoza whose breath reanimates both Machiavellian realism and Marxist critique.

3. SPINOZA BEYOND INDIVIDUALISM

Was Spinoza a philosopher of individualism, a thinker snugly fitting into that particular strain of modernity that the natural law tradition makes room for somewhere between Hobbes and Rousseau? Certain contemporary thinkers are prepared to contend that he was, especially when they focus on the relation that exists in Spinoza between the modal singularities and the more or less constructive expressivity of his ontology. For them the relation between the potencies arises in a flat and neutral manner in Spinoza, as a purely temporary and provisional relation, a transindividual relation, but never as anything more than a relation *between*, in other words, a horizontal relation. Now, even if that were the case, how would one account for the historicity of institutions in the *Tractatus theologico-politicus*, for example? Or again: how would one grasp the formulation of the *summa potestas* in the *Ethics* and the *Tractatus politicus*? In order to supply a response to these obvious objections, our individualist interpreters speak of the process of potency as an "accumulation." This is a key point for them: it allows them to ground and develop a constitutive dynamic that is proper to political institutions and radically critical with respect to the transcendental conception of power proper to the Hobbesian current of political philosophy that held sway in modernity until the Rousseauist turn. The accumulation of the products or effects of social potencies is presented *monistically*, which mirrors the immanentist refusal of any form of "contract" between State and society. Thus our individualist interpreters suppress any possibility of transferring part of immanent potency to transcendental power. To put it even more starkly: by laying stress on the idea of an accumulation of potency, they succeed in sloughing off all the theological ideologies—more or less in the style of Carl Schmitt—that accompany the postmodern restoration of the concept of sovereignty, both on the right and on the left.

So how does accumulation come about? For the individualist interpreters of Spinozism, it comes about through the tendential unification of constitutive potency and juridical positivism. This, viewed from a certain angle, is not false: the tendential unity of *potentia* and *ius* is indeed outlined more than once in Spinoza. But against this potential unity must be set the declaration in the *Tractatus politicus* (chap. 2, section 13, reprising the *Ethics* on this point) that potency grows as the association broadens. There can never be a zero-sum game through the association of the singularities and the accumulation of potencies, for the latter *produce*. But then, how is it possible to maintain both the flat neutrality of the interrelations among individuals, and the ethical enrichment that follows the institutional accumulation of social cooperation? The argument is self-contradictory, inasmuch as the *positive* identity of potency and law [*droit*] can never be flattened in *positivist* fashion.

It is this contradiction that warrants our opponents in their refusal of any finalism or determinism in Spinozan theory. Clearly there is nothing teleological in his ontology. But it is also clear that the defense of liberty constitutes a value for Spinoza, and this defense of liberty indubitably represents the telos of his thought—and even, according to Spinoza himself, that of political activity in general. The question is whether this teleology of praxis can be avoided. And, from the point of view of ontology (but equally that of a very Spinozan "sociology of the affects"), the discovery that the social process is anything but a zero-sum game, that it represents a real collective strategy, requires a material basis. Better yet: it is a process that forces the singularities to pass over into the social ensemble, and that modifies, transforms, and informs collective institutions. Spinozan immanence is itself constitutive. This is what Laurent Bove has very recently shown to great effect.[9] Filippo Del Lucchese has gone on to highlight the reprise of Machiavelli by Spinoza, not under the figure of "Machiavellianism" (that is, of a neutralizing political science, of a positivist formalism, of an apology for force, of a philistine reason of State), but rather as an inexhaustible instance of liberty constructed in resistance and struggle.[10]

Here we come to another essential point about the concept of *potentia*. As the reader will no doubt recall, the constitutive process of *potentia* unfolds through a series of successive integrations and institutional constructions, from *conatus* to *cupiditas* and finally to the rational expression of *amor*. So *cupiditas* stands at the heart of this process. It is in fact the moment where the physical determination of *appetitus* and the corporality of *conatus*, because they are organized in the social experience, produce *imagination*. The imagination is an anticipation of the constitution of institutions; it is the potency that borders on rationality and structures its trajectory—or more exactly: that *expresses* it. Gilles Deleuze calls the thought of Spinoza a "philosophy of expression."[11] It is the imagination that draws the singularities from resistance toward the common. And it is there that *cupiditas* acts—because, in this action, "desire which springs from reason cannot be excessive."[12]

Immanence is here asserted in the most fundamental manner, and the strategy of *cupiditas* here reveals the asymmetry between *potentia* and *potestas*, in other words, the irreducibility of the development of constituent (social, collective) desire to the production (however necessary) of the norms of power. All the theories aiming to neutralize the transformative radicality of the thought of Spinoza and restrict it to a pure individualism manage to avert their gaze from this asymmetry, this excess or surplus or overflow. Yet it is this perpetual excess of liberatory reason that, through the imagination, is constructed between the action of *cupiditas* and the tension of *amor*—on the edge of being, in eternity.

Let me pause here for an aside. All those who make it their business to try to conceal or erase Spinoza's ethical *cupiditas* have the odd habit of grounding their analysis of his political thought on his political texts rather than on the *Ethics*. They need to be forcibly reminded that the political thought of Spinoza is to be found in his ontology, meaning in the *Ethics*, much more than in any other parallel or posterior work. It is precisely on the relation between *cupiditas* and *amor* that all those who wish to neutralize political *potentia* seem to founder—because, to the extent that they push aside the *Ethics*, they forget the existence of this relation; and they remain unaware that that which *cupiditas* constructs as *summa potestas*, *amor* outstrips as *res publica*, as commonwealth. The asymmetry between *potentia* and *potestas* can thus be grasped with the same intensity whether one considers it from above (in the reality of the *cupiditas-amor* bond that exalts its productivity) or from below (when *potentia* is formed and acts in the perspective of an infinite opening).

Let us resume. The individualist interpreters of Spinozan immanentism maintain that in Spinoza the political is a "medium," endowed with ubiquity, and that it therefore cannot be defined either as an element of action or as a property of structure. To me, on the contrary, it seems that in Spinoza the political absolutely cannot be defined as a medium of the social, and that the political is instead both the permanent source and the continual constitutive rupture of the social, a potency exceeding all measure—an excess that is in reality an ontological asymmetry. If this were not the case, we would effectively be condemned to the acosmism of the political, and by that I don't just mean the acosmism of the pantheistic conception of being in Hegel—although I mean that too. For another thing, these interpreters insist on the fact that, in Spinoza, the political can never be instrumental, and that it is constructed in the rapport between individuals and groups, in the complex dynamic that binds them. No doubt they are right. But that does not suffice to qualify the "event" of Spinozan politics. This dialectic (which is not a dialectic) always yields a *surplus* of the constitutive process, as I see it. A *surplus* that is institutive and communicative, and that is thus neither individual nor interindividual; an accumulation not of substantial (individual) segments but of modal (singular) potencies. Spinoza's monism is nourished by the divine potency. Is it not precisely this claim to render divinity *operative*—following a rigorously immanentist line—that makes "the Jew of Amsterdam" a heretic?

It is no coincidence that in Spinoza positive potency and negative potency, "power over" and "power to," are quite indistinguishable: for him there does not exist any static antinomy, or more simply still, from the ontological point of view, *the negative does not exist*. There is only potency (meaning liberty), which is opposed to nothingness and which constructs the common. "The man, who is guided by reason, is more free in a State, where he lives under a general system of law, than in solitude, where he is independent."[13]

What then does it signify "to measure the force of the impact of Spinozan ontology on the traditional conceptual grid of politics"? "The right of resistance, political liberty, sedition, obligations or bonds—and their rational legitimation—are obvious key terms of modern political thought, exactly as they are for Machiavelli."[14] This is how certain materialist interpreters have responded recently—and of course I share their conclusions. The task ahead will be to consider these concepts over the span of time from Machiavelli to Spinoza, while holding them steadfastly apart from modern natural-law doctrine as formulated by Hobbes and Rousseau. What is a democracy, what is a multitude? And what are the "internal trajectories" one must traverse to find an answer to these questions?

Our interpreters choose to give primacy to the thought of Machiavelli and Spinoza. These two authors "represent a veritable anomaly in the first stage of the modern epoch. They construct a rhetorical thought of conflict—a veritable political lineage of *seditio*—that causes the foundations upon which the dogmas of modern politics have been constructed to tremble. Modern politics is, in effect, represented as a thought of order and the neutralization of conflict. . . . On the contrary, the relation between law and conflict, for Machiavelli as for Spinoza, possesses a complex rhythm . . . a recursive relation . . . beyond any dialectical schema of reconciliation and synthesis of the two terms."[15] Del Lucchese, whom we are quoting here, continues by opening his analysis to the postmodern: "in the contemporary epoch, Foucault expressed better than anyone else the conflictual character of history and its amphibious sense: on one hand, as the expression of conflicts, struggles, and revolts . . . on the other, as an instrument of the theoretical struggle through the modern political order. . . . In modern political philosophy, war comes to overlay law totally."[16]

Law [*droit*] is the power of the winner of the war—but nobody ever really wins the war. In consequence, history presents itself as a mass of entanglements and confrontations, in other words, as a dualism rather than as a unitary process; and in truth the rapport between Machiavelli and Spinoza defines the sole paradigm that still allows us to bind future struggles and a future revolutionary project to the past and the present: *seditio sive ius*.

One is therefore obliged to ask: how could all that have been forgotten in the periods of revolutionary political debate nearest to us?[17] How was it possible to force the political under the yoke of a putative "autonomy" and replace Machiavelli with Carl Schmitt? How was it possible to lose the sense of duplicity and ambiguity that characterizes the rapport between ontological potencies and political institutions—or, rather, between the productive forces and the relations of production?

This is the barrier between us and "the autonomy of the political," the representative traditions of the modern constitutional State; this is where the attempt to represent the dynamic force of the political understood democratically, *seditio*, through its contractual and constitutional limitation, falls short. The limit is not in the nature of things but in their distortion.

Del Lucchese continues to work this terrain, seeking to show that the strategy of *conatus* is not grounded in an ontological priority, and that it must be read rather as a rapport internal to the potency of the multitude. "This movement brings out the immanent rationality of institutions: 'ontogenetic point of view of the law [*droit*] of nature and not of the law [*loi*], of potency and not of power.' . . . The law [*loi*] itself is the 'necessary mediation of the potency of the multitude in its affirmation, in the same way that it is the symptom of its present state.' "[18] That means that the institutional process arises from within struggle. It is out of swelling indignation that sedition arises, but it is from swelling sedition that the revolutionary expansion of liberty opens up: there we have the basis from which to oppose the developmental potency of a true revolutionary democracy of the struggles of the multitude against *imperium*. The institution of this democracy rests on nothing that is not internal to this development. "Sedition must be thought as internal and co-existing with law and the State, and may thus be conceived outside any dialectical mechanism. . . . *Libera multitudo* to the extent that *libera seditio*. Behold the monstrous character of the challenge that Machiavelli and Spinoza have launched, in tracing different lines of division within the semantic field of politics. And it truly is a battlefield."[19]

I believe that this reading adds the coherent finishing touches to the one I tried to develop, starting from the same set of problems, in *The Savage Anomaly*. My effort to foreground the concept of *potentia* may sometimes have produced an equivocal effect, inasmuch as it appeared to endow it with a certain anteriority vis-à-vis the concept of power. And if this anteriority were then applied to the analysis of the juridical systems of the contemporary world, there would arise a further risk of equivocation, of conceiving the relation between the constituent power and the formalism of the law in an antinomian manner, of creating a Manichaean tension. May I therefore lay any such equivocation, which was mentioned above, definitively to rest.

Let us turn to another matter. The subversive current of thought at the heart of modernity, from Machiavelli to Spinoza to Marx, drains a whole set of concepts of their meaning and force as it sweeps us from contract to potency and from *seditio* to democracy. Yet today, paradoxically, we see these wisps being reintroduced into the debate through the channel of certain theologico-political experiments (that present themselves as merely hermeneutics but that are really engaged in foundation-laying).

Thus, for example, our good old "modern" age (the modernity of contracts and pacts) is today readmitted and reconfigured by some as a *katechon*, as the experience of necessity, as the force or institution standing as a bulwark against ineluctable evil.[20] I would like to mention here a few contributions that reacted, from a materialist and Spinozan point of view, to this threat once it emerged; and it is with a certain enthusiasm, I confess, that I say bluntly: enough already with this *katechon*! The core of my reasoning is this: once we surrender to the *katechon*, we are no longer engaged in conflict, we slump back onto defeat and its interiorization. Long ago I analyzed certain variants of this maneuver of seventeenth-century thought when it was faced with the crisis of the humanist revolution.[21] Augusto Illuminati has also addressed the matter with great intelligence, moving from Heidegger—he who blocked, in nihilistic fashion, the immanent sense of the movement of being—to the recent revival of the Pauline apologetic for the *katechon*, which seems to recognize the apparition of transcendence on the edge of being. ("Contingency is lived as anguish and resolved through obedience—do we not here detect participation in the movement that resolves being-for-death, once conscious, into Heidegger's great heeding of Being? And is heeding not then the height of obedience?")[22]

"The autonomy of the political." What did this slogan ever signify except the autolimitation of struggle (in the past) and the revival of the theme of "that-which-cannot-be-surpassed" (in the present)—of that which contains within itself its own limit: radical evil? indispensable primitive accumulation? changeless forms and modes of production? In sum: how was this slogan ever interpreted to mean anything except the renunciation of any transformative potency?

On the contrary, the only admissible "autonomy of the political" is that which is produced by the "free multitude." François

Zourabichvili has brought out very clearly the enigma of the free multitude against any individualistic limit. There is no multitude in the "state of nature." There is no multitude before the "civil state." The multitude is not some sort of intermediate concept between individuals and the instituted community. "But then, why is the multitude any more than just a conceptual chimera? By virtue of the natural tension of individuals towards the community (that is, of their common horror of solitude). The logic is familiar: it is that of common notions. The consistency of the concept of multitude is to be found, then, in the tension of a common desire. And it is in this common desire that the institution is grounded."[23] Thus there is only a *multitude-making* [*faire-multitude*, italics in the original], which is equally an *institution-making*, because the making [*faire*] is the very reality of the multitude. From our perspective, there is no multitude but for liberty and in liberty, and there is thus no *katechon* worth anything, and the historical conditions of a free multitude have to do with the fact that the multitude constructs itself in an ongoing manner, in producing common experience and institutions. There is no "State within the State," said Spinoza. We could add: "except for the free multitude." There lies the road of exodus that the multitude, because it conquers liberty and constructs institutions, ceaselessly travels.

This brings us to the next point: starting with a critique of individualism, we have now established a certain consistency in Spinozan thought, which is absolutely irrecuperable within the categories of modernity (if we regard "individualism" as an essential attribute of the definition of what "modern" thought is).[24] The "anomaly" in the thought of Spinoza is not simply an ideal figure capable of utilization in the historical interpretation of his thought; it is a living anomaly that anticipates and can construct a different path for the development of thought and liberty. And one might add here that this path breaks with the theoretical and political will to keep on defining modernity as the indispensable horizon of history. Of these indispensable horizons of history we have had far too many! There is beauty in discovering, without any sort of nostalgia or illusion, a hard foundation for subversive thought: the one that Spinoza offers postmodernity. An irrecuperable thought, a thought irreducible to modernity.

4. THE ALTERNATIVE OF A LIVING MATERIALISM

From the individualistic interpretation of the thought of Spinoza, we must now shift our perspective to meet another challenge: an extremely complex and articulated operation that is trying to guide the definition of the political thought of Spinoza onto ontologically neutral terrain—terrain metaphysically individualistic once again. Metaphysics against ontology. What I mean is that, rather than constructing an individualistic Spinoza by digging into his thought and confronting his ontology in an intensive manner (which is one way of falsifying Spinoza), they advance an individualistic position by drawing upon "modern thought" in general. Shunning any critical, philosophical, or conceptual stance, they present us with a historicizing, encyclopedic profile, in the style of the "history of ideas."

As a result we are offered the figure of an individualistic Spinoza as an *ideal-type* of modernity. On this view, Spinoza becomes a modern tout court: he is modernity and not an alternative within modern thought or in relation to it. It is not just Hobbes and Hegel who are modern: Spinoza is too. Even better, he is both modern and subversive. Margaret Candee Jacob[25] and Jonathan Israel[26] have worked this seam. They are excellent historians, but the ground they are treading is full of landmines they cannot recognize. Their shared insistence on the "making of modernity" is the badge of the hypothesis they strenuously maintain: the philosophy of Spinoza is the foundation of the radical Enlightenment and Spinozism represents the living structure of the age of Enlightenment. Unhappily, this thesis will not hold up, and is in part false. I shall not enter here into the details of the controversy; from the point of view of strict historiography of philosophy, Laurent Bove has subjected it to a review both benevolent and harsh.[27] And from the point of view of historiography tout court, it has been critiqued—and in fact demolished—by the remarkable analysis of Antoine Lilti.[28] For my part, I have no doubt that Spinozism does indeed include a line of radical philosophical polemic taken up by atheists and pantheists, freemasons and republicans, throughout the prehistory of the French Revolution. But that is not the problem that the philosophy of Spinoza poses.

The problem that Spinoza poses is whether, at the heart of modernity, there exists the possibility of democratic thought, whether there exists the hypothesis of government by the multitude, whether the institutionalization of the common is possible. It is the problem of whether it is possible for these elements to eventuate in immanence, in contradiction to the assertion of sovereign transcendence. Or: it is the problem of the possibility, the necessity even, of grounding the ethical (and the ethical-political in particular) in bodies, in the materiality of desire, and in the fluxes of their encounter and their clash. It is the question of the manner in which love, which rips us free of solitude and permits us to construct the world together, can be imposed as the rationale of this development.

It is evident that fragments of this type of reasoning do turn up from time to time over the history of modernity, before and after

Spinoza. What I am trying to show is that such political reasoning, Spinozan after a fashion, was never dominant (was indeed very much in the minority) in the centuries from the crisis of the Renaissance to the French Revolution, and on to the worker insurrections of the nineteenth century. The stream of political reason that did prevail was that of Hobbes, Rousseau, and Hegel: from the point of view of political philosophy, we know of course that they were individualists and hence contractualists; but it is just as evident that they were opportunists, transcendentalists, and dialecticians as they strove to ground sovereignty. And it is clear that modernity constructed itself here on the synthesis between bourgeois individualism and sovereign power. Descartes, more than anyone else, shed light on the importance of this dichotomy while reasonably enclosing the contradiction within the cloistered walls of theology.[29] Spinoza does not even take this dialectic into consideration. His stance is located radically outside it. But he is *outside* modernity because he is *beyond* modernity. Radical individualism is foreign to him. What he disdains in contractualism is what he would have disdained in the materialism of the Enlightenment—because Spinozan materialism is a far cry from the wretchedly individualistic, mechanistic, and physicalist materialism of the thought of the eighteenth century. Spinoza's materialism is much more akin to the fresh and vital force of the materialism of a Bacon, or to the (still humanist) materialism of a Machiavelli or a Galileo. That is all; there is nothing more. Spinoza is an alternative to modernity; he is inside modernity only in order to train his gaze on values that modernity precisely cannot express, because it has excluded them from its own foundation.

It is important to pay attention here. The question of Spinozan materialism goes well beyond the dimensions and figures of Enlightenment materialism (from this point of view, only Diderot is truly Spinozan), but it has never been approached with clarity. Quite the contrary: because the terms of the comparison have been reversed, and the materialism of the Enlightenment has been taken as the paradigm, there is generally a hesitation (and of course it could hardly be otherwise) to attribute materialist characteristics to Spinozan immanentism, as though materialism could never be any different from the particular version of materialism, polemical and mechanistic, that is proper to the eighteenth century (and, by extension, to the nineteenth). Now, this particular materialism (here I am thinking specifically of the nineteenth-century version) is either the plebeian product of an anticapitalist and antireligious polemic, or the tenacious residue of attempts to constitute a metaphysics of science. If one's point of departure is extravagant in that way, then of course it seems difficult to imagine the possibility of conjoining immanentism and materialism. But did the hylozoism or the ontology of the pre-Socratics not present, however primordially, this articulation? And did the passage from Epicurus to Lucretius not take place along this axis of thought? Or again: in late scholastic Aristotelianism at Paris and at Padua, and in the maturation of European humanism right at the core of modern thought, do we not find precisely this vivacious materialist immanentism working to achieve an interpretation of the new potency of life?

The effort by Spinoza to draw from this secret current of ontology (which grounds modernity but does not succeed in fully realizing itself in modernity), his capacity to defend its outlets even from within the failure of the Renaissance (and humanism) against the triumph of the baroque (and sovereign absolutism), and finally, his reproposal of the religion of liberty through articulation between the singularity and the community (against individualism)—all this makes the immanentism and materialism of

Spinoza impossible to fit into the structures of modernity, while opening it up to the *postmodern*.

One last remark. In the 1960s and 1970s, we lived through an epoch of profound crisis of socialist ideology, and of self-critique by Marxist thought. Perhaps today we can rediscover the Spinozan origins of this reflection. A simple example: when Althusser posits a radical "caesura" in the development of Marxist thought, he does not yet think that the solution of the rupture between the scientific methodology of the mature Marx and his initial humanism can be interpreted in Spinozan terms. But later, at the most radical phase of his post-Marxist conversion, he does suggest something of this kind, and makes it a decisive element in his reworking of his own materialism.[30] This allusion to Spinoza on Althusser's part is extraordinarily telling. It signifies that Spinozan immanentism can finally liberate us from all forms of dialecticism, from all teleology; that his materialism is not narrow, but aleatory and open to the virtualities of being; that through the avowed articulation between immanentism and materialism, knowledge will henceforth rely on resistance, and happiness on the rational passion of the multitude.

This is why, when the tableau of the struggle for the emancipation of mankind widens, and the critique becomes that of the development of capitalism in its postmodern phase (when it really subsumes society; capitalism in its imperial, postcolonial phase), the Spinozan "matrix" palpably overrides the Marxist "caesura." What is clearly voiced here is a materialism of ontological dispositifs, of the production of subjectivity. And it is a historical shift encompassing all those who have constructed a thought of difference that begins with emancipation and is both antiteleological and immanentist. This is the moment at which the new materialism of Spinoza starts to yield its fruits, and where it shows us—through the articulations of substance—the productivity of the modes, that is to say, the singular and revolutionary fold that each of them presents.

Let us sum up. The analyses that seek to foreground individualism in the thought of Spinoza are no more able to position Spinoza within the broad mainstream of modernity than are the more or less teleological "history of ideas" approaches. That he lived in the seventeenth century and therefore in the modern era is certainly true, but only in the chronological sense. Spinoza actually opposes—or more precisely, he sets his ontology against—all the paradigms of modern thought. From our perspective, he represents an alternative to the modern, an interruption within his century; and he beckons to us today from the postmodern. Not out of the potency of the individual, but out of the potency of the common and of love.

5. WHO IS AFRAID OF A POSITIVE ONTOLOGY?

With the constructive aspects of the political ontology of Spinoza firmly stated (and their fundamentally anti-individualistic bias emphasized), we must now try to understand how a certain amount of counterfire has been directed at this ontology—in other words, against a positive and productive conception of being. This counterfire reacted not so much to the reading of Spinoza we have just been discussing (and that we naturally defend), as against the theoretical and political effects of the Spinoza renaissance.

The first counterblast, then: the Platonizing attempt, endlessly rehearsed by theologians of the most petulant kind in their campaign against the "damned Jew," to portray substance in Spinoza as compact, undifferentiated, and incapable of articulation.

Nietzsche demolished this type of reading with ironic relish. Yet today we have Alain Badiou raising the same theological hue and cry, and posing as the ultimate champion of this interpretative stance.[31] As early as *Theory of the Subject* (1982), Badiou wasn't shy about attacking both Althusser and Deleuze in the same fashion, despite claiming them as his masters, on account of their interest in Spinoza. And if he did grant some moral value to Spinozan "audacity," it was only so that he could immediately set up a vulgar comparison between Spinoza and Malebranche, in the most sarcastic manner imaginable. Badiou's text leads the reader to assume that by 1982 he was acquainted with Malebranche, and we may suppose that he was. But it is plain to see that the readings of Spinoza produced after 1968, and echoing 1968, were still as remote from him then as a distant galaxy; no doubt he read them later. Yet in *Deleuze* (1997) he still portrays Spinoza as unrecognizable in Deleuze's reading of him (and this despite his own attempt to bring Deleuze into the Maoist orbit). In his *Briefings on Existence* (1998), Badiou finally explains himself in detail on the whole question. He first denies that the event could open up to heterogeneous multiplicity, then accuses Deleuze of defending, in his reading of Spinoza, an (irrationalist) ontology of the forms of becoming, and Spinoza of developing a closed ontology, shut in on itself. It is interesting to note how Badiou's ontology of the event shuns any materialist reference and takes refuge in an ideology of communism for which only the mystical affirmation *credo, quia absurdum* can account. It is the return of Malebranche.

And it gets better. An Italian philosopher (half-Platonic and half-Heideggerian in his approach to Spinoza) feels compelled to insist on the drastic alternative between God and nothingness. Hence, Emanuele Severino (for it is he) informs us, when Spinoza excludes divinity from the substance of religion, he must inevitably tend toward nothingness![32] One would dearly love to know why. Severino naturally endorses the traditional view that Spinoza's philosophy represents "the most radical and alternative system in the history of Western philosophy since Jesus Christ"; but, as reactionary historians of philosophy often do, precisely so as to neutralize this potent alternative radicality, he adds that Spinozan immanence inclines toward nothingness, that the absolute of production appears to be confused with that of destruction, and that these opposing drives "share the decisive and abyssal conviction that the things of this world are nothing." The most sophisticated form of this effort at neutralization was probably that elaborated by Hegel, who first asserts that "one cannot philosophize without being Spinozan," meaning that only immersion in the absolute, and the absolute itself, open the portals to philosophy, but then immediately adds: not only is Spinoza incapable of developing this absolute character because he is not a trinitarian or a dialectician, and because he is Jewish: he is also incapable because he was only a "poor consumptive" who lacked the strength to do so. What a joke! Yet polemics of this sort keep recurring, and allow those who see in being a tendency toward death to make a show of reproaching the author who wrote, "a free man thinks of death least of all things; and his wisdom is a meditation not of death but of life,"[33] with confusing being and nonbeing. And yet: "We may add that our mind, in so far as it perceives things truly, is part of the infinite intellect of God."[34] Thus it possesses the potency of the divine: this nature, this matter of which we are made, does have that potency.

Let us pick up our thread. Since our horizon at the moment is the history of the manifestations of Spinozan potency, let us ask ourselves what the materialism of Spinoza might be today, and in what form it might present itself to us. It is not, to start with, a materialism of the inert object, any more than it is a materialism arising out of necessary causal sequences. On the contrary, it is a materialism of active differences and subjective dispositifs, that is to say, an assertion of matter as productive force, through the activity of those modalities that constitute substance. Since 1968 this line of interpretation has pervaded the whole territory of readings of Spinoza, and it seems hard to conceive how anyone could be a Spinozan today (or in the future), by which I mean how one could even just begin to think, if one denies the impact of what he achieved. It was in opposition to the tendency to view substance as the One, and more generally against attempts to neutralize the potency of Spinozan being, that the article that appears as chapter 2 below was written. And to cast one last glance back at Badiou: what an antimaterialist he must be, to be so set against Spinoza!

There is a third and last aspect of the attacks on Spinoza the secular materialist that I cherish especially, more refined than the previous ones, no doubt, and just as dangerous. It does not challenge the productivity of being in Spinoza; and the internal articulation, the degree of mobility, and the alternatives within the necessary determinations of being in Spinoza are certainly taken into account. But what is refuted is the very possibility of traversing the ontological horizon of Spinozism from its base—or better, from below.

Let us see how this works. The main thing as far as the authors I have in mind are concerned is to critique all the strong interpretations of Spinoza's project for a *democratia omnino absoluta*.[35] As far as they are concerned, to adopt this perspective would actually amount to transforming Spinoza's materialism into a philosophy of history. This sort of critique rests on a few pillars. One is the claim that the new trends in the interpretation of Spinoza, especially that of Deleuze, supposedly employ the *mos geometricus* as a means of making Spinozan ontology dynamic and antihierarchical. The other is that the Foucauldian conceptual vocabulary is being used to try to turn the relation between *potentia* and *potestas* into a new binomial, "biopolitical activity/exercise of biopowers." The result is depicted as an absolute antinomy between an (ontologically creative) *potentia* and a (parasitical) *potestas*. While the critics are right to note the theoretical convergence of thought-worlds like those of Deleuze, Foucault, and my own from the political point of view (and for Deleuze and me: on the basis of our interpretation of Spinoza), it is precisely for that same reason that it is a mistake to push the *potentia/potestas* relation to an antinomic limit. The dichotomy between biopolitics and the biopowers, both of them coexisting eternally, exactly like labor and capital, is presented in terms both open and chaotic in Deleuze, and is constructed in genealogical fashion in Foucault. What else, for that matter, could the "accumulation" of potencies be? Simply the action of *potentia* both *within* and *against potestas*.

In *Empire* and *Multitude*, and especially in our recent *Commonwealth*, Michael Hardt and I laid stress on what is both an interaction and a dissociation between *potentia* and *potestas*, between biopolitics and the biopowers. Through a reprise of the "habit" dear to American pragmatists, and of *habitus* in the sense Bourdieu gave the word, what we have done is retrace the stages of the (internal) constitution of the rapport and the difference between *potentia* and *potestas*. The antinomy of the two effects (that is, the two characters) of potency cannot be defined as ontological dualism: it is a contrast that never ceases self-producing, a conflict that continuously takes place and is continuously resolved and immediately re-forms at another level, an ethical tension that emerges through the difficulties and obstacles of the trajectory that is sketched out on the basis of *conatus*, traverses *cupiditas*, and arrives at the expression of *amor*. If the rapport between *potentia* and *potestas* is subsequently recognized as "asymmetric," that is possible only because *potentia*, as *cupiditas*, can never become bad, and because it always contains an excess. What is bad is what is not realized. Moreover, *potentia* constructs the common, in other words, it actually directs the accumulation of the passions in the direction of the common. It is through a permanent production of subjectivity that it conducts the struggle for the common, and leads it toward an amorous consciousness of rationality.

The second pillar on which these critiques rely is the claim that there is a juridical and positivist element in the way we evaluate the development of potency in Spinoza. The authors ranged against us seem to think that if absolute democracy is allowed to stand on our terms, the implication it leads to is an unjustified interruption of the ongoing process that brings individuals and social forces into conflict, and that characterizes the ethical terrain in Spinoza. Now, I sincerely believe that the juridical effectiveness of institutions cannot just be characterized in Spinoza as an indistinct "conduct of conducts," nor even that the relation between the political constitution and the juridical system is posited within a static relation, or, to put it another way, under conditions of technological efficiency. Spinoza is not Luhmann; the constitution in Spinoza is always a *mover* and not a result, a "constituent power," a permanent source of law; and thus the juridical system only becomes effective through the continual action of the constituent potencies.

Let me end with a few remarks on the trajectory of one of the greatest interpreters of Spinoza, and probably one of the founders of postmodern Spinozism, Alexandre Matheron. Matheron is seen as a pupil of Martial Guéroult, a great example of philological virtuosity if ever there was one. But that filiation is nonsense, because the philology of Matheron always had a political soul, and because it has, by virtue of that, rendered political the *bifurcation* that was created in modern philosophy starting with Spinoza. The same bifurcation also appeared in philosophy after 1968, when Spinozism blossomed afresh against Heideggerianism, making it possible to stress political realism against Heideggerian mysticism in philosophy and Schmittian cynicism in politics. Let me stress once more the importance of the rediscovery of Spinoza in the 1970s: at the moment of farewell to traditional Marxism, it was Spinozism that made it possible to refuse all the variants, "strong" or "weak," of the thought of *krisis*.[36] Instead of celebrating, with a frisson of anguish, the need to restore order and submit to the rude exercise of the economic arms of capitalism, instead of accepting a conception of being within which the memory of a formidable epoch of struggle could be drowned, it was possible to start to rebuild, on the terrain of Spinozism, a revolutionary perspective. Because, as Matheron and his students taught,[37] being is a means for the destruction of sadness, desire is a dispositif for the collective construction of liberty and joy, and "absolute democracy," the democracy of struggle, is the only conceivable form of liberty and equality.

6. OF WHAT USE IS SPINOZA TODAY?

We have already answered the question in part. No doubt it needs to be done more meticulously. Contemporary materialism has been caught up—essentially as ontology and as politics—in the turbulent shipwreck of "real socialism." Yet this collapse was prepared not just by the dogmatic precipitation of Soviet *dialectical* materialism, but (and perhaps with even greater intensity) by *critical* materialism in its Western version. I refer to the critical materialism of the Frankfurt school, the school of totalizing alienation and reification, the school that did not discern the "real subsumption" of society under capital: a conception without alternatives except maybe the terrible one of terrorism, a triumph of what has been called the "pessimism of reason."[38] Nothing can escape the advance of capitalist power. Free markets, imperial globalizations, the destruction of the guarantees of the welfare state were the result (immediately picked up by bourgeois political theory) of these eschatological conceptions passing themselves off as critical. The paradox was that, to save us from this abyss, the only available guidance was often that furnished by the propaganda of the "Heideggerian shepherd," or by a whole series of other mystical expectancies. Numerous poststructuralist philosophies have found a niche on the margins of society subsumed under capital, and have, at best, offered us a repetition of Benjaminian despair— or, at worst, brandished the specter of a repetition of the horror of the Shoah. So how to get out of this nightmare?

Yet between Deleuze and Guattari on one hand, and Derrida and Foucault on the other, there was a way out. In Foucault, this egress assumed the form of a new horizon of the production of subjectivity within the tissue of biopolitics.[39] Body, biopolitics, subjectivity: here we have the contemporary equivalents of *conatus*, of *appetitus* with a modal horizon, of *cupiditas*, and of *amor*. It is here that, with the desperate monism of the capitalist absolute cast off, Spinoza springs back to life, and depicts, at the forefront of the philosophical stage, the possibility of breaking with that murderous world. When Matheron assumed his stance in this context of analysis, he had already done original and remarkably profound work, in his *Individu et communauté*, on the role of the sentiments in the production of institutions, the formation of the State, and the determination of the ontological condition of human cooperation;

and he had developed this schema as a function of the history of the West. In *Le Christ et le salut des Ignorants chez Spinoza* (1971), Matheron sent forth fresh filaments of research.[40] These filaments are, as Chantal Jacquet nicely puts it, "that of time, duration, and eternity; that of potency and action; and finally that of the rapport between the body and the mind."[41] Each of these themes deserves a long commentary on its own, in the wake of the formidable investigations carried out by Matheron and his students. But once again I would simply like to stress the way in which materialism, when placed under the logical and ontological lens of Spinozism, is able at last to abandon its traditional dialectical status, and how it can, on the contrary, endow itself with a project both constitutive and subjective. In so doing, it molds itself to our time, and the new figure of the class struggle corresponding to it. This turn is not to be taken lightly, if only because it sets a materialist analysis of the political against both a dimension of the theologico-political that never ceases to reemerge, and the recurrent reproposals (from the right, of course, but also, more and more, from the left) of politics as sovereignty and, as Jacques Rancière puts it, as "policing."[42] It is time to be done with these theoretical illusions, if we wish to construct a political horizon of liberty.

The question then arises: how do we follow Spinoza on this terrain? Where is this productive rapport and how can it be identified? And above all: who guarantees the positivity of the production of the common on the part of the multitude? What proof is there that the multitude, instead of being productive of democracy, isn't just a mob, a pure upsurge of plebeian disorder? Is this not where the sin of "optimism of the will," so characteristic of Gramsci and Italian Marxism, gets committed?

Well, it seems to me that the choice set before the multitude by certain authors (from Manfred Walther to Étienne Balibar)[43]—

either resign yourselves to being a mob, or be a true movement of liberation—constitutes, if one takes it very concretely as an ethical indication, a sort of philosophical muddle. What is the basis of the a priori claim that the multitude could transform itself into a mob rather than into a liberation movement? It is true that Spinoza denounces the *ultimi barbarorum* of the unreasoning and murderous mass; but he immediately goes on to specify that it is "the fear of the masses" that generates barbarities. It falls not to us but to the multitude itself to decide what it wants to be. Every individual has far too often behaved like a scoundrel before turning his desire toward the multitude. Besides, if we examine this choice from a theoretical rather than a practical perspective, what we have before us is really nothing more than a simple proposal of transcendence—a countermove against Spinozan ontology. They pretend to be offering an alternative, while presenting us once again with the Hobbesian alienation of sovereignty as the only conceivable option. Because it is perfectly easy to see what the actual content of this offered choice is: it is juridical positivism in general. And juridical positivism is a lot closer to the philosophy of history of Hegelianism or of positivism (to the extent that it participates in the exaltation of things as they are) than it is to the ethical experimentation to which Spinoza invites us. I for my part think that through a deeper engagement with materialism, the guarantee of a "march of freedom" can emerge through the study of the transformations of labor, production, technology, and the effects all that may be having on political anthropology.

I quite fail to see why there is any need to be talking about "philosophy of history," when one is in fact talking, very concretely and from a strictly immanentist point of view, about "production of subjectivity." Objectively viewed, this production of subjectivity is fully grounded and materially constructed—indeed, it has

sometimes even taken place. It is the social conditions of our existence that confirm this reality for us. The theory of the multitude
(and the eventuality that the multitude might accomplish a "march
of freedom") arises simply out of the observation of the development of material civilization. What is here being proposed in a
Spinozan manner is an alternative of struggling against exploitation and seeking happiness. With that point established—that our
arguments are material and objective—it should be added that
any nonphilistine philosophy, any philosophy not totally stifled by
ideological reticence, must decide—as Spinoza intended—where
to stand: on the side of the oppressed or on the side of the oppres-
sors. Let us recall here that the "pessimism of reason and optimism of the will" promoted by Gramsci has nothing to do with the
matter at hand, because, from a Spinozan perspective, only "the
optimism of reason" is active (and perhaps on occasion a certain
"pessimism of the will").

The last argument of my critics: some of them pretend to wonder whether this tension toward absolute democracy is really anything more than a cloak for another political theology. The critics
put it this way: Negri and his friends must admit, at any rate,
that the multitude, being a problematic concept, cannot guarantee its own "good" development, in other words, it cannot certify
that it will be drawn to "the good." Faced with this stance, what
am I to do? Choose "absolute" democracy—a democracy that is
no longer a "form of government," but the management of the
freedom of all by these *all* themselves. Very well, say the critics,
but since politics is inconceivable without sovereignty, Negri is
obviously talking theology when he talks about absolute democracy (and the democratic multitude); the Spinozan perspective is
actually one of conflict without end that can never find a willed or
determined solution. Isn't Negri just reaching for an "ontological

guarantee," utopian and unavailable, for the collective emancipation of humanity? Isn't what Negri is peddling just a political theology, plain and simple?

It is, on the face of it, scarcely worth the effort to respond
to these contorted imaginings; nevertheless, I shall try. What
exactly does "political theology" mean anyway? I for my part am
acquainted with just one political theology, the one at whose opposite and symmetrical extremes stand Bodin and Stalin, with Carl
Schmitt occupying a slot somewhere in between. A political theology denies any possibility that the political order of the collectiv-
ity might be torn away from the One, from the "God on earth."
That is the Western definition of what a political theology is, and
it applies equally to the Catholic, socialist, and fascist variants.
In Spinoza, conversely, the theory of absolute democracy is the
attempt to invent a new form of politics that makes a clean break
with the theory of sovereignty and the classic tripartition of the
theories of the government of the One. If, in Spinoza, the absolute is the ontological tissue of the free singularities, it is realistic
to think—and he does, in fact, maintain as much—that power-
potestas is the result of the effort to limit the action of the singularities in their quest for liberty. On that basis, I believe that the
social movements that are trying today to challenge *potestas* and
act in affirmation of liberty are following Spinoza's proposition to
the letter. If anyone wants to qualify that proposition as "theological," let them do so, as long as they have no fear of ridicule. But
let them at least quit pretending at the same time to have real
benevolence for Spinoza, since his thought, with its irremediably
subversive and *maledicta* character, resists recuperation by means
of theological compromise.

Let me end with a word or two about the equivocations of what
is generally called "political realism." Even if one accepted the

view that politics is no more than the effort to regulate a perennial interindividual conflict, even from within the horizon of "political realism" so-called—why is this terrain of conflict regarded in such a flat way? Why are the libertarian tensions played out there damped down so drastically? Why is the possibility dismissed that struggles for liberty might be capable of producing new subjectivities and anthropological metamorphoses? Machiavelli, with his own humanist realism, always retained this positive outlook; in *A Thousand Plateaus*, Deleuze and Guattari showed its activity; Foucault, particularly in some of his Collège de France courses, began to construct this process of production "from below." The claim that a theory of *potentia* can only be "diagnostic, critical, and explicative" robs Spinozism of its very essence as a theory of *cupiditas* and rational *amor*, of liberty and of the common.

The four texts assembled here have been selected from among the ones I have written since the collection *Spinoza subversif* (1994) because I regard them as particularly well suited to support the interpretive theses briefly sketched out above.

Chapter 1 is a lecture delivered at the Spinozahuis at Rijnsburg on 27 June 2009. Since the setting was a Spinozan sodality and the occasion celebratory, I discuss the "fortune," the afterlife, of the Spinozan anomaly, attempting to bring out its critical and subversive implications for late modern thought and the contemporary epoch, and to read in it certain anticipations of the philosophy of the present.

Chapter 2 is a paper delivered at the ninth international meeting of the Spinoza-Gesellschaft at the Humboldt-Universität, Berlin, on 30 September 2006. The purpose here was to exalt the Spinozan "time of potency" in contradistinction to the Heideggerian "impotency of time," and to stress the hypothesis of a new Spinozan composition of the time of postmodernity. The role played by Nietzsche, a reader of Spinoza, in the definition of the new ontological compositions capable of challenging Heideggerianism is stressed.

Chapter 3 is a paper delivered at the international conference *Spinoza as Social and Political Thinker* organized by the Jerusalem Spinoza Institute on 31 May 2007. Since the topic was absolute democracy, I aimed to stress the monist characteristics of democracy, the intensity of its immanent genesis. It is indeed not unusual, in Israel and elsewhere, to come across exegetes of Spinoza who interpret the absolute character of the democratic constitution in theological, indeed sometimes overtly theocratic, terms. I try to show that, on the contrary, in Spinozism the rapport with history makes it possible to give depth to the concept of democracy.

Chapter 4 is a text presented at the colloquy *Spinoza et les sciences sociales* at the Université de Paris-VIII on 9 April 2005. It is meant to specify the movement in the thought of Spinoza that makes it possible to ascend from the social to the political, from the refusal of solitude to the construction of the multitude, and to *multitude-making [faire-multitude]* as the institutional device for the affirmation of the *common*. The aim is to show how the Spinozan anomaly can become part of our social life, and its capacity to supply democratic politics with constant nourishment—without ever having to normalize itself.

ONE

SPINOZA

A Heresy of Immanence
and of Democracy

Some time ago now, when I was working on the political under-
tones in the thought of Descartes, I provided an outline of what I
called the "reasonable politics" of the ideology of modernity,[1] plot-
ting its different lines of development and range of alternatives.
Recently I have returned to the topic, comparing my own reading to the new readings of Descartes that have appeared over the
last thirty years. And I have found my earlier theses confirmed.
These focused on the genesis and development of early capitalism, and the choices made by bourgeois ideology at a time when
it was attempting to construct political forms corresponding both
to primitive capital accumulation (through the construction of the

absolutist state), and to the formation and long-term consolidation of the third estate in that context.[2]

As everyone knows, a privileged place was occupied within the "reasonable ideology" of the third estate by the organs of repression required to put down rural and urban revolts (revolts by craftworkers who were really just proletarians) when these revolts threatened capitalist development. No matter where on the spectrum of political thought one stood, some reference to transcendence was required in the age of Descartes in order to underwrite absolute sovereignty and the efficacity of its action. Power, which was being organized in the bosom of capital and which allowed and stimulated its development, had necessarily—or rather, given the intensity of the resistance it encountered, *could not not*—root itself in the absolute of transcendence. Theological necessity had, in that age, totally permeated the development of capital and the philosophies of the present: this is precisely how the ontotheological metaphysics of modernity was instituted.

In other words, when the modern world was opened up to capitalist development, the *new productive forces* (above all living labor) had to be subjected to an old eternal figure of power, to the absolute character of a power capable of legitimizing the *new relations of production*. From that moment on, any attempt to challenge this state of affairs was regarded as damnable and heretical, and any aspiration to modify this general framework was only acceptable if it touched on the relations of production in a highly theoretical and moderate manner, and with a very prudent lucidity. This is exactly what Descartes did. So part of my task was to register the degree to which modern metaphysics (and when one speaks of metaphysics one is also always speaking, one way or another, about theology) honed and reinforced its political pretensions. From then on, metaphysics has always been political.

It was within a climate governed by such moderation and reticence that the theory of power develops in the modern era. The political thinkers of transcendence become hegemonic. The modern theory of sovereignty is born with Hobbes. Bodin had already tried, with all his well-known intelligence—for what he in effect maintains is that every form of government is logically monarchical. Monarchy covers both aristocratic government and democratic government, because both of them are governed by the principle of the One. Consequently they are monarchic, whatever the hypocritical cloak of legitimacy donned by power. But we have to wait for Hobbes for the citizens as such to become fundamental in the construction of the absolute character of power. What we have with Hobbes is a transfer of the potency of civil subjects to the sovereign.

It is a strange thing, this transfer of the potency of the citizens to the sovereign. Why does that have to happen? Because of the English civil war? But isn't it precisely with Leviathan, which enables sovereign power to come into existence, that civil society itself is enabled? So then how can there be a civil war prior to civil society? And as if that fairytale weren't enough, Hobbes can always fall back on the divine potency that overrides and legitimizes the power of Leviathan. Genuine civil war of the kind that primitive accumulation had unleashed (and the surplus of violence that the expropriation of the common had provoked)—is that what the critical gaze is being trained on here? No, not that at all, and without any critique either: everything is immediately justified, rendered necessary and legitimate simply by the theological power of the sovereign.

But there was more. It was not enough to impose sovereign rule and so make the surge of capital possible; subjects had to be stripped of the ability to recognize their own singular potency; the expropriation of that potency and their consciousness of their own

alienation had to be justified by a state of necessity; and finally, all
the justifications for an eventual rebellion, for possible resistance,
had to be suppressed. Alienation thus becomes inevitable and
paradoxically advantageous. The construction of this condition
represents the essential axis of the political theories that develop
around the transcendence of sovereignty. The shift that takes place
is *the invention of the public*. The expropriation of the common
that developed during the process of primitive accumulation is
transfigured and mystified through the invention of public utility.
In this context, the theory of the general will in Rousseau is in a
certain sense perfectly intelligible.

And it was on this basis that Hegel accomplished his synthesis
of the public and the sovereign, of command and progress, through
the dialectical *Aufhebung* of civil society into the State—completing
in fact the necessary subjection of living labor to sovereign power.

And yet the modern era saw the rise of another strain of philosophy that takes form and grows quite differently. It is a thought
that cohabits with the struggles, with the revolts, with the revolu-
tions that recur throughout modernity. It is a thought that fore-
grounds the rule of immanence, that is incarnated in a politics of
immanence. The position is absolutely clear if you contrast the
thought of Spinoza with that of Bodin and Hobbes. For them, as
we just saw, any government is necessarily the government of the
One. For Spinoza, in contrast, if there were no more democratic
conatus there would no longer be any State; and without democracy there is no longer any political life or authority: monarchy
is always naked, meaning incapable of absolute sovereignty and
contradicted by the citizens; and aristocracy is lame in the same
fashion. It is only immanence that can produce the polis.

But how to understand the notion of immanence? Immanence signifies that this world here has no *beyond*; that it is only possible

to live (move, create) *inside* this world, *here below*; that the being in which we find ourselves—and of which we cannot free ourselves because we are made of it, and because all the things we do are no more than an *acting upon our being* (which is also always *our being in action*)—I was saying, that the being in which we find ourselves is an open becoming, not a closed one, that it is not prefigured or preformed, but is on the contrary produced. If we put ourselves, in Sartre's phrase, *en situation*, may we thereby conclude that the relations of production do not dominate, but are dominated by, the productive forces? I believe so profoundly. We are in the situation exactly contrary to what the political theorists of transcendence were prescribing, which was that the relations of production—the fact that one born a slave must necessarily die a slave—constitute a necessity guaranteed by the goodness of God. If, as the theologians and political theorists tell us, the power of man over man is in the DNA of creation (please pardon that image), then it becomes imperative to respond that immanence is *being-against*.

Then we start to detect striking "anomalies" with respect to the main modern tradition of sovereignty: exceptions and ruptures that are posited by the thinkers of immanence at the core of the history of modern political thought. Machiavelli anticipates a conflictual theory of power by reversing in advance the civil war theory that Hobbes will use, in a naturalistic and contractual fashion, to construct his own theory of absolute power—in other words, by pretending to refer to a history of individualistic and proprietorial relations. No, says Machiavelli, the conflict is always ongoing, power is always a rapport, there are winners and losers—but let's not tell ourselves fairytales: he who has power is simply he who has greater force. Now, if all that is what our own experience tells us, then it necessarily follows that power cannot exist without a subject, and that command can only ever come about *over* or *against* a resistance. Theoretically this resistance can always topple the power in its turn. And if that is the case, is the door not then open to a *democratic theory* of power?

It is here that Spinoza steps in.[3]

Spinoza tells us that society has no need of power in order to be constituted. Only the subjects can construct society—or better still produce, through insisting on the potency of singularities, through the passions that traverse the multitudes, all the forms of the State. And any form of State can be legitimated only by the relation that is woven between the subjects and the sovereign, or vice versa, between the sovereign and the subjects. There is no "sacred history," other than the narration of this very human thing; and if a God does exist, it is one whom the desire for happiness invents through the movements and transformations of the multitude. In Spinoza, the productive forces produce the relations of production. But inasmuch as the forces of production are in all respects *cupiditates*, forces of passion, multitudes open to the constitution of the political, we have verification of what Machiavelli's theory had already anticipated back in his day: the forms of command are subject to the activity of the multitude.

In Marx, finally, the pairs conflict/becoming and production/ potency are reconciled through the critique of political economy. Marx gives *meaning* to this "exceptional" process that the anomalies of modernity have produced—and his meaning is communism. It would be profoundly mistaken to confuse this political meaning with some telos in history, however. In Marx it is struggle that molds the visage of institutions, it is the forces of production that produce and eventually overturn the social relations within which they are paradoxically clamped and restrained.

After Marx, the alternatives to communism will often attempt to realize themselves on the terrain of immanence as well. Transcendence appears to be permanently ruled out. Even the grand synthesis of Hegel (transcendental from the start and before very long transcendent too, following the rhythm of the absolute spirit) is caught up in the whirlwind of the materiality of historical processes—of struggle, resistance, revolution—in which the political theorists of immanence express themselves. And the political theorists of immanence express themselves in a manner that the sovereign finds increasingly alarming. So a sense of propriety and prudence demands that the alternatives realize themselves on the terrain of immanence as well, since it appears to have prevailed completely. But beware: this terrain has been tampered with. Immanence has become a new fetish, in the name of which are presented to us theoretical experiences that, *against* communism, surreptitiously reintroduce into political discourse this idea of necessity, which blocks and denies the processes of liberation and the effectual practices of liberty.

Kant—a philosopher all too often associated with idealism, whereas in fact he is essentially a man and an author of the Enlightenment—had foreseen, in his *Conflict of the Faculties*, that out of the affirmation of liberty, and beyond liberty, new instances of repression of the forces of production would emerge, in the definition of the historical process, in the organization of its finalities and in the structures of power that would flow from it. And he added: these will be reactionary experiments.

Let us pick up the hint Kant drops for us, let us try to classify some of them.

First of all, there are the experiments in "Abderitism" (atomism). We are talking here of an opaque materialism that reduces the world to an ensemble of irrational contingencies, combinations of circumstances (in the context of a metaphysical necessity dominating existence), and that consequently subordinates historical development to a deterministic finality. This is what Louis Althusser, for example, sometimes does when he likens hazard and necessity. Now, long before Althusser, and with much less elegance and conceptual suppleness, so-called scientific socialism and dialectical materialism were formidable examples of this manner of utilizing immanence so as to eliminate, paradoxically, the ontological creativity that represents the most salient trait of the "abnormal philosophies" of modernity, in other words and once again: the mark of liberty. Note that when I speak here of liberty, I am speaking not of spiritual essences but of resistance and rebellion, directly entailing imagination and invention. An invention not so much of souls as of bodies, of cooperation, of new forms of labor. How many tragedies of knowledge and of the political will unfurl within this horizon in the decades that lie ahead?

Let us return to Kant. Kant says on the other hand that there is "terrorism." What does this word signify for Kant? For him, it is any theory that posits that revolution is impossible, and thus terrorizes people by holding them in thrall to the presence of death, by pointing it out to them as their inevitable destiny, and by flattening their every desire beneath the weight of the shadow of death. A far cry from Kantian thought, this position and the authors who embody it constitute a second group that gives rise to experiments that mystify immanence in the twentieth century. The passivity that necessity entails, and the listlessness that springs from the uncertain consciousness of the inevitable defeat of desire, indeed the complacency maintained vis-à-vis this condition, represent the mark of a new ethic of transcendence on the scene of contemporary philosophy. From Heidegger to the weak and marginal variants of the postmodern, reactionary ideology waxes today under these forms. We are at the antipodes of a thought of immanence of the sort whose birth we have sought to pinpoint in the theoretical clash that characterized the origins of modernity: anomaly, exception, rupture.[4]

What a heap of other charges of this kind could be laid at the door of this broad reactionary lineage. Not, of course, the histories and philosophies, the practices and ideologies, that led to the horrible atrocities of fascist or Stalinist terror, but tendencies that are often hegemonic from the rhetorical and political point of view, and whose essential meaning is a sense of impotency, even an incapacity (aspiring to be critical) to express any force whatever. Some of these positions (think, for example, of the works of Jacques Derrida or Giorgio Agamben) try to present themselves as heretical stances, opposed to the dominant ideology. But they are a far cry indeed from how they imagine themselves. Heresy is always a break in the order of the branches of knowledges, or more precisely a positive overflow, the product of a theoretical invention expressing itself with creativity and thus exalting the ontological singularity of the present. But what we encounter in the stances mentioned above are weak, marginal variants, ethically otiose. Or else we meet wonder, more or less aestheticized, at the sublime. We meet the beauty of life, we meet flight from struggle, we meet contempt for historical determinations, we meet libertine-destructive skepticism taking the place of overflow and true resistance. It is the triumph of the sad passions.

Second point: "heresy" signifies the refusal of transcendence in all its forms, so it is likewise a disagreement about just what a concept might be, because the heretical concept is no longer even trying to be universal, but common. Heresy refuses to accept the habits of command and instituted knowledge, and, knowing well their ends, it resists them in critical fashion. The heretic is the intellectual moved by a specific, particular point of view, which is not that of totality but of rupture, and which thus constructs the figure of a situated knowledge and an action conditioned by a common project of resistance and struggle. It is precisely there that the overflow of heresy can begin to open itself up . . . open itself up to what? To a generous construction of the common.

So we arrive at a crucial element that may make it possible to distinguish clearly the political theorists of transcendence from the political theorists of immanence.

But before going deeper into what *the common* is, allow me to draw attention in passing to a group of heretics—among so many others—who did, so to speak, build a bridge between the critique of modernity and the philosophico-political configuration that obtains today. I wish to dwell for a moment on this strange subversive thought that, in France, and through a thousand rivulets very different among themselves (from *Socialism or Barbarism* to situationism), has introduced us to the joyous inventions of Deleuze and Guattari, and to those, more arduous politically and more complex in their fashion, of Michel Foucault. I purposely leave out that other collection of "kernels of subversive thought" that worked in the same period—in places different again, but in a highly coherent manner—on the construction of this heresy, which has been mine as well, and which permitted us to live the experience of communist struggle and the exercise of libertarian passion: Soviet critical thought built around the refusal of dialectical materialism and around a different management of Soviet planning; Italian workerism; certain currents of colonial and postcolonial thought; and so on. We ought to pay more attention to all these authors—not just on the terrain of political debate, evidently, but also from the point of view of the construction of a new philosophical horizon.

Some aspects, then, of French postwar thought that I have just qualified as "subversive." There are certain pages of Maurice Merleau-Ponty, for example (I am thinking of texts from the collection *Signes*, and the formidable preface to that volume dated February-September 1960),[5] that seem to clarify, from right inside the class struggle, what the redefinition of a horizon both critical and creative might be. I refer to it here to demonstrate what the place of criticism, or more exactly of a "point of view" that chooses to wield the philosophical arm of immanence, might be. When we rebel, Merleau-Ponty tells us, referring explicitly to the uprising by the workers of Budapest, we do so not in the name of liberty of conscience or philosophical idealism; on the contrary, being Marxists, in other words, because we are inserted into a precise combination of circumstances, in a given situation, we choose rupture. We break with a universe to which we wish to give a meaning that is *other* and *new*. The Hungarian workers in question, Merleau-Ponty goes on, have rejected a certain idea of being-object, and have thus introduced the critique of socialist identity and a practice of difference which is that of free men, singularities in struggle—a practice of constituent rebellion. They have adopted the conception and the practice of a being that has numerous dimensions, a sort of "multiversus," a produced being, collectively constructed. The problem of whether one ought to take a stance inside or outside the party, or more exactly to place oneself inside or outside concrete history, in reality depends absolutely on a common action that violates the rule and reinvents history. Being-object, being-subject: these are so many barbarisms from which we must hope we will soon be liberated—even if it becomes necessary to invent others. In the short term, our task is to reveal the potency of common action, if indeed it exists. And if we can, it is precisely because authors and militants have trod this path and have given to this expression of resistance both elementary and strong the materiality of a *production of subjectivity*. These are instruments of organization, tendencies that link the future awaiting construction to the hazards of present struggles; these are sketches of a joyous future that deconstruct the violence of present suffering. We are not men of the dialectic, but we are not helpless men either—and every stance we take is *disutopian*, affirmative, constituent.

So it is no coincidence, as Merleau-Ponty reminds us in the preface to *Signes* when speaking of Paul Nizan, that "many Marxists have been drawn to Spinozism." The reason is that the thought of the infinite makes it possible to break free of necessity and reinvent the world. Is that an audacious conclusion? Not really. Think of it as *a method that makes it possible to move between historical determinism and the ontology of creative potency*, that makes it possible to be *en situation* without losing the capacity to effect rupture. To confront the real world critically, to determine a course of action that traverses the real world in critical fashion. Today, no doubt, we would be inclined to critique Spinoza's way of employing the notion of infinity, and favor instead the infinitely more Spinozan notion of eternity, but it is hardly a matter of importance.

If we fast forward a bit and train our gaze on the patch of history we are living through now, there is one more thing to add: who would ever have thought that a proletarian movement could really be defined in terms of *Bios*? That a political struggle for liberation could arise and express itself in terms that concern the whole of life—or as some would say, the whole *biopolitical* context, the whole interwoven fabric of the bodies and institutions of common life? Who would ever have thought that this perspective would one day arise from the strong affirmation of a strong and irreducible *point of view*? From a specific act of imagination "within" a vital process of struggle? Irreducible: not because this point of view is adapted to a specific, determinate, hence true, causality, but because it is practical and because it is produced by the instruments of a creative potency. What happens here is what happened to Moses: you will recall the passage from the *Tractatus theologico-politicus* where Spinoza shows that the way in which Moses built a constitution for the mutinous Jewish people who had left Egypt could not have been grounded in fear, but that it had to rest on hope, in other words, on a strong act of the imagination.

Hence we no longer find ourselves in an abstract condition (for example, facing the metaphysical alternative of necessity versus liberty), but rather in a historical condition of life where resistance and the constitution of the common offer themselves as the terms of a tension that must be resolved.

Let us take up our place in this condition, therefore, and let us identify the different directions, or the different deviations, that lie open before us. Gilles Deleuze, for example, plunges into a condition of this type. One could say the same of Guy Debord. And yet the answers the two of them give to the same question are totally different. Deleuze asks: aren't we forced to admit that resistance is "outside" history? His response ultimately is that the "minority" *is never* outside history, because the minority is the same thing as concrete resistance. For Debord, in contrast, resistance is indeed "outside," an extraordinary event. For him, resistance is joyous; it is history that is sad. Of course, in Deleuze too there is the lure of an "outside" that reappears from time to time—in the form of certain discourses on psychosis, on the experience of schizophrenia, on the emergence and the overstepping of the limit. Sometimes the tone is almost naturalistic. Deleuze and Guattari in search of use value? At times it almost seems as if we ought to suppose as much, in other words, that the illusion of being able to attain a fixed point, a measure, something that would save us in every case, persists in defiance of everything in great philosophy. So at times the reasoning seems to curl around itself in expectation of an epiphany. The event undervalues history. But things like that remain episodic. In the course of their grand philosophical "recitation," the main thing Deleuze and Guattari accomplished was to reinvent the concreteness of *disutopia* and interweave the passions of creative subjects with the actuality of struggle and confrontation. Immanence: what will that actually be when theories of transcendence, practices of obedience, and the recognition of identity have all been subverted?

To put this question is not to backtrack, not to revert to analyzing the metaphysical rapport between necessity and liberty. On the contrary, we already locate ourselves totally in the perspective that makes *the ontology of actuality* the basis of *the production of subjectivity*. There is no nostalgia here for the "outside"; by now we are totally "inside." There is no appeal to "use value"; we are by now fully immersed in "exchange value." Is that a bad thing? No. That is reality, that is our life. It is in this "inside," historically situated here within, that we may present the *reappropriation* of "use value" as a central objective. The potency relation admits no other expression today.

Note that "use value" possesses great dignity. It is a common reality: constructed and consolidated in such a way that it can no longer be brought back to the world of pure exchange; it comes about under a common form. The product of labor has become solid. It is there. There is nothing else, there is no "outside." Take today's financial world for example: who could imagine doing without it? The world of finance is by now similar to the earth— what is happening to it is what happened to the common lands expropriated at the start of the modern era: it is a common reality, in which we were living, and which was taken away from us. So we want to take it back, this "earth."

Spinoza explained to us the importance of the Jubilee in Jewish history: it was when all debts were canceled and the material equality of the citizens restored. Think too of Machiavelli, who insists on the centrality of "agrarian laws" in the history of the Roman republic—when sovereignty inclines before the democracy of the producers through plebeian reappropriation of the land. Think about these cases. We must not view "use value" with nostalgia. On the contrary, it is fundamental to recognize that we are living in the world of exchange, of merchandise and its circulation, and that we have no need to attain—or more exactly, to go back to—anything pure and primal. All we wish is to keep on rebelling, here and now, enmeshed in this reality. Freeing ourselves of exchange value will thus mean reappropriating for ourselves the common reality (this reality that was created both by labor and exploitation, by cooperation and profits/sales, each of these terms playing simultaneously within and against its "other"). Reappropriating for ourselves this common reality which we are producing and which they never stop trying to turn back against us in the form of power. Overturning this reality that makes us live as "poor-exploited" and "subjects" in the "common of valorization," in the "communism of capital." Reappropriating it for ourselves on the contrary as the "common of living labor."

We have been circling around the problem. Let us not be surprised if we feel ourselves for the first time capable of truly expressing the problem of the common. Not the common that was ripped away from us at birth by primitive accumulation—and with what pain! Not simply the "use value" of the labor force, but the new consistency of the value of labor—multiplied by the experience of struggle and by the common reappropriation of knowledge.

A new common. A common that goes beyond private appropriation and public appropriation, and that strides forth today as a subject of struggle against the public powers, which are really no more than an instrument of the private. *The common against the public.* The common is a surplus, a potency that mankind has constructed, and that it can go on constructing in the gesture that frees it from command and exploitation. The common is both the milieu in which occurs the rupture that we are constructing against the power that dominates us, and the result of this rupture. Consequently an ontology of actuality comes into being at the moment at which subjectivities produce and construct themselves in the common—more precisely, at the moment at which the multitude of singularities discovers in the common the sign of the constructive efficacity of being. It is only through the deconstruction of sovereignty, of the subject/figure of transcendence, that the multitude succeeds in constructing the common. *A democratic construction?* Yes, as long as we believe that the multitude is not a "particular configuration of circumstances" [*une conjoncture*] but a *cupiditas*—the tension of countless singularities within an ever-open process of constitution, in an uninterrupted effort to constitute the common. The multitude is an endlessly vivacious *ensemble of institutions.* The Spinozan analysis of the history of the Jews is not alone in showing us that. There is also the philosophical anthropology that emphasizes the ongoing processes of transformation between the ontology of actuality and the production of subjectivity. *Potentia multitudinis!*

And so we arrive at the conclusion of our modest reasoning, which began in the modern era with Machiavelli and Spinoza (and no doubt with many other thinkers, prophets, and henchmen) in rebellion and resistance, that is to say, at the moment at which criticism attempted for the first time to assert *the dominance of the productive forces* over (and against) the relations of production. Today at last these productive forces know that it is entirely possible for them to set themselves free of power and the relations of production. There you have the immanence to which Deleuze was referring. Not a thought of eternity, dissolving into the infinite, but a potent action realized in an exact and absolute manner. There you have the soul of the politics of immanence: political action acquires meaning through the recognition of the common, or more accurately through the explicit construction and production of the common.

Let me end by returning to the philosophical proposition advanced in *The Savage Anomaly*. What it proposed is the insurrection of *potentia*. The constitutive process of *potentia* develops in Spinoza, as we know, through successive integrations and institutional constructions, from *conatus* to *cupiditas* and on to the rational expression of *amor*. At the center of this process stands *cupiditas*. *Cupiditas* is the moment in which the physical character of *appetitus* and the corporality of *conatus*, organizing themselves in social experience, produce imagination. The imagination is an anticipation of the constitution of institutions; it is the potency that arrives at the edge of rationality and that structures its journey, that *expresses* this advance. Deleuze called Spinoza's thought a "philosophy of expression." It is the imagination that draws the singularities and makes them pass from resistance over to the common. And it is precisely there that *cupiditas* acts: for, in this action, "desire which springs from reason cannot be excessive."[6] There we have immanence declaring itself in the most fundamental manner, where the strategy of *cupiditas* shows the asymmetry between *potentia* and *potestas*, the irreducibility of the development of constituent (social, collective) desire to the production (albeit necessary) of the norms of command.

It is this asymmetry, this excess, that all the theories whose business it is to neutralize the transformative and radical nature of the thought of Spinoza attempt to efface: the perpetual overflow of this liberatory reason that, through the imagination, constructs itself between the action of *cupiditas* and the tension of *amor*—on the edge of being, in inventing eternity.[7]

All those who attempt to neutralize the ethical *cupiditas* of Spinoza have a strange habit: they ground their analysis of Spinoza's political thought in his *political* texts rather than on the *Ethics*. So it should be stressed, in conclusion, that the political thought of Spinoza is to be found in his ontology—in the *Ethics*—much more than in any parallel or posterior work. It is over the relationship between *cupiditas* and *amor* that all those whose goal it is to neutralize political *potentia* stumble, for in setting aside the *Ethics* they forget that that which *cupiditas* constructs with *summa potestas*, *amor* drives further still, and outstrips as *res publica*, as *commonwealth*. The asymmetry between *potentia* and *potestas* can thus be grasped with the same intensity, whether one considers it from above (that is, through the realization of the *cupiditas-amor* link that exalts its productive character), or whether one regards it from below, where *potentia* takes on form and acts in the perspective of an infinite opening.[8]

I conclude, then. The political, in Spinoza, is not a generalized mediation of the social. It may, on the contrary, be defined as a utensil for action, as an active and transitive property of the social structure. If the political is not a *medium* of the social in Spinoza, that is because it is rather its permanent source, because it represents the constitutive break ceaselessly relaunched: a potency that exceeds all measure, an overflow that is an ontological asymmetry—because if it were not, we would, it seems to me, really be condemned not just to the acosmism of the pantheistic conception of being, as Hegel thought, but to the acosmism of the political.

Second point. If, in Spinoza, the political can never be instrumental but on the contrary constructs itself in the dynamic rapport between individuals and groups, in the dialectic (which is absolutely not dialectical) between singularities and common, there is always a *surplus* that comes about in relation to the constitutive process. A *surplus* that is institutive and communicative, that is thus not individual nor interindividual, not an accumuluation of substantial (individual) segments, but an articulation of modal (singular) potencies. Spinozan monism is nourished by the divine potency. And it no doubt is this—the fact of rendering God not otiose but *busy*, of putting him to work—through a rigorously immanentist option that makes the Jewish philosopher of Amsterdam a "heretic."

Third and last point. Positive and negative potency, "power to" and "power over," are not in the least distinct in Spinoza's thought. Understandably, because there exists no static antinomy in Spinoza; but also, and especially, because, from an ontological point of view, *the negative does not exist*. In Spinoza there is only the potency, in other words, liberty, that is opposed to nothingness and that constructs the common. "The man who is directed by reason is more free in the State [*civitas*], where he lives according to the common decree, than in solitude where he obeys only himself."[9] That is the lesson of Spinoza.

| TWO |

POTENCY AND ONTOLOGY

Heidegger or Spinoza

The real, or what Hegel calls modernity, is the immediate unity of essence and existence, of the inner and the outer, in form and in dialectic: there you have it, the stormy cape around which philosophical critique has been struggling to make headway for almost two centuries. It looked as though Hegel had achieved a resolution of the problem. But during the silver age of contemporary German philosophy, and even more in its bronze age (the nineteenth century and fin-de-siècle period of "critical critique" and great university philosophy), essence and existence, substance and potency—Germanized as *Wirklichkeit* and *Da-Sein*—drifted ever farther apart. Substance, once thought of as effectual reality, came to be seen as power and destiny. Potency was now similarly banished to the realm of the irrational, where once it had been experienced as antagonism. Philosophy gradually mutated into an attempted display of sublimity, a way of exorcising the irrational, while potency was simply manipulated. First a duality was posited between, on the one hand, crisis and the tragic horizon of thought and, on the other, the energetic Hegelian drive to ground the dialectical hegemony of absolute substance. Then philosophy assumed the perpetual vocation of renewing all the old transcendental teleologies in some more or less dialectical mode, and despite the withering irony directed at them by such greats as Marx and Nietzsche, it continued to project one image of modernity after another onto its shifting horizon, each as pretentious as, and even more languid than, the one before.

The hegemony of the relations of production over the productive forces begets its own representation of the Hegelian utopia of the absolute, the triumph of the modern (capitalist) State in other words, and drapes it in reformist teleology. The schemas of indefinite duration, played against those of the dialectical infinite, are revived as projects for a rationality of progressive power. The end of history becomes the finality of history. Modernity changes the sheets but doesn't change beds. Philosophy's progress grows halting, it exhausts the possibilities of any real renewal of thought one after another, it seizes on a thousand expedients in order to circumvent the very dry, very illusory, very sure-of-itself, and very utopian Hegelian intimation of modernity, replacing it with the worn and tattered forms of the schematism of reason and transcendentality. To the point where this reflection self-consumes and spills its own vacuity over the very definition of being.

Heidegger represents the extreme tip of this process, nor is he in any sense alien to it; indeed, the reformulation of the

Kantian theory of transcendental schematism is boldly proclaimed as one of the purposes of *Being and Time*. Yet the very moment he sets about reworking the familiar themes, his reprise totally convulses the process. "Our aim in the following treatise is to work out the question of the meaning of *being* and to do so concretely. Our provisional aim is the interpretation of *time* as the possible horizon for any understanding whatsoever of being."[1] But: "If the interpretation of the meaning of being is to become a task, Da-Sein is not only the primary being to be interrogated; in addition to this it is the being that always already in its being is related to *what is sought* in this question. But then the question of being is nothing else than the radicalization of an essential tendency of being that belongs to Da-Sein itself, namely, of the pre-ontological understanding of being."[2]

The theme of present time, of its relation to being, and thus of its singular effectuality is thus foregrounded. But here, contrary to what Hegel had tried to construct, *Da-Sein* is a temporality broken apart and then rediscovered in every respect as presence: a presence that is stability and singular rootedness, in contrast to the dispersed consistency of *Man*, in contrast to disorientation of any kind. Becoming and history are henceforth no more than a destiny of commerce and friability. Effectuality is no longer Hegelian *Wirklichkeit*, but rude *Faktizität*. Modernity is destiny. In the final pages of *Being and Time*, against the mediation and the absolute spirit of Hegel, Heidegger asserts: "Our existential analytic of Da-Sein, on the other hand, begins with the 'concretion' of factically thrown existence, and reveals temporality as what makes such existence primordially possible. 'Spirit' does not first fall into time, but *exists as* the primordial *temporalizing* of temporality. . . . Spirit does not fall *into* time, but factical existence 'falls,' in falling prey, *out of* primordial, authentic temporality."[3]

Here, in this fall, in this "care," temporality is constituted as possibility and self-projection into the future. Without ever exposing itself to the danger of teleology and the dialectic, temporality reveals the possibility of presence as the most originary ontological determination of *Da-Sein*. It is only in presence that destiny opens anew to possibility and the future. But how to authenticate *Da-Sein*? Amid this tragic muddle, death represents the most authentic and appropriate possibility of *Da-Sein*. But death is also the impossibility of presence: the "possibility of an impossibility" thus becomes the most appropriate and authentic determination of *Da-Sein*. It is then easy to conclude that the fundamental theme of Hegelian modernity—the synthesis of being and time, of *Wirklichkeit* and *Da-Sein*—has now ended. Or better, that it has been reversed: it is in nothingness, in death, that the immediate unity of essence and existence comes about. Hegelian claims for the historical *Bestimmung* of singularities have become *Entschlossenheit*—deliberation and resolution of the opening of *Da-Sein* to its own truth, which is nothingness. The little tune that drove the dance of determination and the transcendental has ended.

With Hegel and Heidegger, we thus have two experiences opposed to life—because after having underlined its own possibility of existence within the power of the dialectic, the bourgeois property of happiness discovers that it is inconsistent. Even the later Heidegger, following the *Kehre*, will not succeed in modifying this situation. The distance between Hegel and Heidegger could not be greater, meaning the distance between Heidegger and the whole of modern philosophy. And yet paradoxically Heidegger is not all that isolated. He is not simply the prophet of the destiny of modernity. At the very moment at which his function is termination, Heidegger represents a portal that can open onto antimodernity, meaning onto a conception of time as ontologically constitutive relation, which breaks radically with the hegemony of substance and of the transcendental, and opens it on the contrary onto a sort of potency. The theoretical decision consists not only in affirming closure (*Entschlossenheit*); it is related to anticipation and opening, which are truth itself inasmuch as it unveils itself in *Da-Sein*. The discovery of being means more than just the fact of disclosing (*Ent-decken*) the preexistent; it means posing the autonomous stability of *Da-Sein* through and against the dispersive mobility of *Man*. In its finitude, *Da-Sein* is open, and this opening is vision (*Sicht*), but, more than vision, it is an *Umsicht*, a 360-degree circumspection and indeed a fore-spection too. *Da-Sein* is a possibility, but more than that, it is a power of being. " 'We' presupposes truth because 'we,' existing in the kind of being of Da-Sein, *are* 'in the truth.' "[4]

And again:

> But Da-Sein is always already ahead of itself; that lies in its constitution of being as care. It is a being that is concerned in its being about its ownmost potentiality-of-being. Disclosedness and discovering belong essentially to the being and potentiality-for-being of Da-Sein as being-in-the-world. Da-Sein is concerned with its potentiality-for-being-in-the-world, and this includes circumspectly discovering and taking care of innerworldly beings. In the constitution of being of Da-Sein as care, in being ahead of itself, lies the most primordial "presupposing."[5]

Presence then means not simply the fact of being present in truth, the unconcealed character of being, but the projection of the present, of authenticity, of the new rootedness of being. Time aspires to potency, it alludes to its productivity, it brushes against its energy. And when it does fold back upon nothingness, it nevertheless does not forget potency.

With this we may return to Spinoza and essay the counterintuitive task of linking the philosopher of Amsterdam to Heidegger. *Tempus potentiae.* The Spinozan emphasis on presence fulfills what Heidegger bequeaths us as a mere possibility. The hegemony of the singular presence in the face of becoming, which characterizes the metaphysics of Spinoza vis-à-vis that of Hegel, is reaffirmed as a hegemony of the ontological plenitude of the present as against the empty presence of Heidegger. Without ever having set foot in modernity, Spinoza here exits it at a single bound, in reversing the concentration of time—which Hegel and Heidegger wished to see as concluded, whether in becoming or in nothingness—into a time positively open and constituent. In the ontological condition of this absolute immanentism, love takes the place of "care." Spinoza systematically reverses Heidegger: to *Angst* he opposes *Amor*; to *Umsicht, Mens*; to *Entschlossenheit, Cupiditas*; to *Anwesenheit, Conatus*; to *Besorgen, Appetitus*; to *Möglichkeit, Potentia*. In this opposition, presence, antifinalism, and possibility unite that which the different meanings of ontology divide. And at the same time, the meanings of being undergo a dichotomy—toward nothingness for Heidegger, toward fullness for Spinoza. The Heideggerian ambiguity that vacillates toward the void is resolved in the Spinozan tension that conceives the present as plenitude. If, for Spinoza as for Heidegger, modal presence, meaning the phenomenological being [*l'étant phénoménologique*], is delivered into liberty, Spinoza, unlike Heidegger, perceives a productive force in this being. Hence the reduction of time to presence is carried out in opposite ways: constitution of a presence that goes toward nothingness for Heidegger, creative insistence on presence for Spinoza. Through this reduction to presence, then, two different constitutive directions occupy the horizon: Heidegger may have accounts to settle with modernity, but Spinoza—who lived in modernity but never entered modern philosophy—shows us the indomitable strength of an antimodernity completely projected toward the future. In Spinoza, love expresses the time of potency, a time that is presence as action constitutive of eternity. Even in the very difficult and very problematic genesis of part V of the *Ethics*, one can see this conceptual process unfolding. First, the formal condition of identity of presence and eternity is given: "Whatever the mind understands under the form of eternity, it does not understand by virtue of conceiving the present actual existence of the body, but by virtue of conceiving the essence of the body under the form of eternity."[6] This is repeated by proposition XXX: "Our mind, in so far as it knows itself and the body under the form of eternity, has to that extent necessarily a knowledge of God, and knows that it is in God, and is conceived through God."[7] The relevant explanation is found in the corollary of proposition XXXII: "From the third kind of knowledge necessarily arises the intellectual love of God. From this kind of knowledge arises pleasure accompanied by the idea of God as cause, that is, the love of God; not in so far as we imagine him as present, but in so far as we understand God to be eternal; this is what I call the intellectual love of God."[8]

Eternity is thus the formal dimension of presence. But we are immediately offered an explanation and a reversal: "Although this love towards God has no beginning, it yet possesses all the perfections of love, just as though it had arisen."[9] We must therefore beware of falling into the trap of duration: "If we look to men's general opinion, we shall see that they are indeed conscious of the eternity of their mind, but that they confuse eternity with duration, and ascribe it to the imagination or memory which they believe to remain after death."[10] On the contrary: "This love of the mind must be referred to the activities of the mind; it is itself, indeed, an activity whereby the mind regards itself accompanied by the idea of God as cause; that is an activity whereby God, in so far as he can be explained through the human mind, contemplates himself accompanied by the idea of himself; therefore, this love of the mind is part of the infinite love wherewith God loves himself. QED."[11] "From what has been said, we clearly understand wherein our salvation, or blessedness, or freedom, consists: namely, in the constant and eternal love toward God, or in God's love toward men. This love or blessedness is, in the Bible, called Glory, and not undeservedly."[12] Spinoza's argument concludes, beyond all equivocation, with proposition XL: "In proportion as each thing possesses more of perfection, so it is more active and less passive; and, conversely, in proportion as it is more active, so it is more perfect."[13]

The time of potency is thus constitutive of eternity, inasmuch as constitutive action inheres in presence. The eternity presupposed is here revealed as a product, as a horizon of affirmation and action. Time is a plenum of love. Heideggerian nothingness is met with the Spinozan plenum, that is to say, the paradox of the eternity and plenitude of the present world, the splendor of singularity. The concept of modernity is indeed corroded, but not by "care." By love.

And yet points of contact or commonality between Heidegger and Spinoza may nevertheless be adduced. We have seen— Nietzsche showed it before the whole world—that both of them shatter the myth of modernity. That is what two authors as unlike one another as they could possibly be nevertheless have in common: the rupturing of modernity. How to express this common dimension—this passage through a common perception and experience? Where can we locate an irreducible resemblance?

The first element of the shared introspection in which Spinoza and Heidegger engage on ontological terrain consists of radically affirming being as being-with (*mit-Sein*). There we have the common step that the two philosophies take. With the one and the other, being presents itself as being-with. Of course, it is important not to trivialize this *mit-Sein*: it invests all contingent relations and different figures of linguistic circulation at once. Neither the "weak" philosophies nor the "linguistic" philosophies have really understood it. The milieu into which singularities are plunged—the phenomenological tissue of existence—is in fact a tissue of hard relations: we have the vertiginous impression of being in a pre-Socratic experience of being. "Being-with" is a continuous opening not just toward alterity but toward depth, the inexhaustible instance that the two philosophies reveal. Husserl had already described this immersion of individuality in *mit-Sein*, from which it emerges as singularity. In Husserl, this dimension presented certain aspects that were viewed (or denounced) as vitalist. But it is there, on the contrary, that the phenomenological condition of the plunge into being commenced to present being as a biopolitical figure. We are warned to be careful when we link being to *Bios*; it is true that numerous misunderstandings have fed on it. But, let us repeat, these misunderstandings are the same as the ones we have charted to this point: the alternative between the void and the plenum, nothingness and potency, death and life. That holds good for the rapport between Heidegger and Spinoza: in Spinoza, being takes on a biopolitical figure when his research tends toward "being-multitude," or "making-multitude." Here, being is a productive, absolute immanence. The profoundest depth becomes the surface of existence.

To return to this figure of being leaves an impression on one. Let us remember what Hegel said: without radical Spinozism, no philosophy. Must we join the ranks of those whose claim is: without Heideggerism, no philosophy? It is a claim seemingly embedded in the very experience of the postmodern, and the expressions or definitions of it. But we need to go beyond such claims, and have the courage to add that in Heidegger being is qualified in a scandalous and perverse manner, whereas in Spinoza being is qualified—radically—as potency and hope, as the ontological capacity to produce.

So is it a case of Heidegger the reactionary and fascist versus Spinoza the democrat and communist? Such a crude sketch characterizes Spinoza improperly and unhistorically while forcing Heidegger to bear the guilt he (indisputably) does bear. But it is precisely in order to illuminate this historiographical difficulty (for Spinoza) and on the contrary to make it explicit in relation to the history that Heidegger (as a reactionary) interprets that we assume the risk, and that we go even further and pose a few more questions.

Being in the *mit-Sein* signifies being in the philosophy of the present. The great divergence, the Copernican revolution of contemporary philosophy, is between Husserl and Wittgenstein. Vitalism takes two forms: the mystical perspective constituted by Wittgenstein's linguistic analysis, and the ascetic perspective constituted by Husserlian philosophy. It is through this alternative that the immanence of "being-with" and that of "being-in" are affirmed. To do philosophy is to recognize that we are immersed in time. And there is only the rapport with the other to buffer us against the immediacy of the plunge into the time of being; there is only the sense of difference (the relation among singularities) to draw us out of this condition. The sense of difference itself acts on interaction, in "being-with" and in "being-in."

In this situation, Heidegger and Spinoza make different choices, which Nietzsche, with all the contradiction of his thought, was able to state with clarity before anyone else: one can choose between love of life and adhesion to death, between the pleasure of singularity and that of totality; one can exert the hatred of death against the eternal return, or one can exert the experience of the multitude against the transcendence of the political.

What is amazing is how these different choices, made at a time of profound historical uncertainty, correspond to the historical determinations and the political alternatives that postmodernity will later propose. In fact, Spinoza and Heidegger reason within the "real subsumption of society under capital." If, for Spinoza, it is a question of a theoretical fiction, a projection of the imagination, for Heidegger on the contrary it is an irreversible tendency. For the one and the other, there exists no concrete alternative to this condition, because their respective philosophies are philosophies that have no more "without." Certainly, Heidegger often vacillates; he heeds this appeal of destiny that draws him toward unknowable zones and accentuates a mystical strain within the experience of being: *amor fati*. For Spinoza it was repugnant to behave in that way; his time and his spirit were open to a democratic revolution and pushed him toward the choice of liberty, and thus of acting, of praxis and the capacity to transform interaction into multiplicity and the multitude into democracy. Thus we arrive at the point where the two lines of phenomenology (that of "being-in" the phenomenological context, and that of experimentation with "being-with") intersect and construct a contradictory whole: a whole that is split by different choices.

On one hand, we have Heidegger, who grasps human activity as abstract labor, and man as responsible for this subsumption of life under the power that annuls the freedom of life in transforming it into a product of destiny. On the other, we have Spinoza, who constructs a thought of the materialist reappropriation of labor, of the rupture of the totality of power, and who is the prophet of the democratic constitution. Liberty, for Spinoza, is the very product of desire. If men were born free, they would have no need of good or evil, and there would exist neither wealth nor poverty: it is because man is born miserable that his desire constructs liberty, and, with this liberty, defines the good—whereas evil is only the result of a privation of liberty. And so, once again and in a converse manner, we have Heidegger, who maintains that man is born free but that it is precisely his freedom that brings him to the *impasse* of choice; that freedom is always an excess, that "being-with" is something that ranges men against one another, as if mankind were living in a cage. Spinoza: *cupiditas* is never excessive because freedom is an overflow of being that constructs its own measure when it constitutes itself as history. Heidegger: freedom is "being-for-death."

Such are the two different forms of "phenomenological being" ["*l'être phénoménologique*"; quotation marks in the original] in the exclusive horizon of immanence, of "within." On one hand, reason and affect as the construction of this being; on the other, *Entschlossenheit* and "care" as experience of subjection to a being that reveals itself as alienation and nothingness. On one hand, that which is constructed, the projectual, that which is historically determined; on the other, the *Ur*, the unveiling, nothingness.

Nothing is more disruptive of the postmodern than that opposition. If Spinoza is with Heidegger when it comes to considering the phenomenological dimension as fundamental, he is against him when he develops the potency of the being that is in being present [*l'étant qui est dans l'être présent*], within it as "modality" of life. The degree to which Nietzsche had understood the depth and the potency of this alternative deserves emphasis once again. In fact, Heidegger essentially believes he is borrowing from

Nietzsche this "ideological battering," this flirtation with conservative thought that is typical of a reactionary choice. But, contrary to what Heidegger thinks, there is nothing in Nietzsche that thrusts toward reaction. It is not wrong, in certain cases, to contrast a destructive and ironic Nietzsche and a smiling and good-humored Spinoza; some people have done so, and indeed I have done so myself, but let us leave it at that. Irony versus humor, nature/material (by now stripped of its necessity and tragically open to passion and dispassion) against nature that constructs and plays "prudently," and even goes forward with courage . . . to what extent are such oppositions useful and just?

In comparing Heidegger and Spinoza, matters stand differently. Let me summarize what I have been saying, and how I see the great rift within the philosophy of the twentieth century. On one hand, Heidegger and Spinoza propose to us a return to earth, an exit from any transcendent or transcendental illusion, a recognition that being belongs to us, we who constitute it, and that this world is a tissue of human relations. Is this vitalism? Vitalism takes many forms. The first is the one that makes it the milieu and dimension from which to begin the analysis of being, and that bewilders us with the illusion that being in life signifies being in truth and in the illusion of truth. The second is the one that runs from Dilthey to Husserl, and that expresses itself as the necessity of the phenomenological plunge of the subject into historical being. But perhaps this is already going beyond vitalism. Vitalism is more a conception of being in life that seizes the singularity, in terms of event and epistemology, of *Da-Sein*. Spinoza had delved into this process of being and Heidegger did everything he could to destroy its meaning.

We have thus examined, with too much *equi-proximity* no doubt, the possible points of contact between Heidegger and Spinoza.

This does not mean that we should not denounce the thought of Heidegger as reactionary, and not just because it is probably linked to the vicissitudes of the Nazi movement and fascist politics, but also because its conception of being makes destiny the suffocation of life. Heidegger is a black serpent, he strangles us.

To revert to the Spinozan perspective also enables the formulation of certain prudent reflections on the folly of the human species that the thought of Heidegger interprets or reveals. It allows us to set against Heidegger a conception of being-with (*mit-Sein*) as a dimension both unremarkable and strong of human life. More than anything else, probably, democracy needs this Spinozan prudence of life.

| THREE |

MULTITUDE AND SINGULARITY IN THE DEVELOPMENT OF SPINOZA'S POLITICAL THOUGHT

My task will be to sketch the development of the notions of multitude and singularity in the thought of Spinoza, but I beg the reader's indulgence for a small digression first. In preparing this paper, I was forced to pay heed to certain authors who have found a niche for themselves in recent years in the international philosophical gazettes and in academic publishing. What their discourse boils down to is the radical refusal of the relationship or rapport between the singularities and the multitude. Such a relation, at once open and perfectly essential, lies at the core of the democratic Spinozism of circa 1968, from which my own reading of Spinoza naturally springs, and which is the real target of their refusal. So I shall take this opportunity to respond—in glancing but quite explicit fashion—to these new interpretative tendencies and to reaffirm the democratic stance to which I continue to adhere. This may entail some infidelity to the strict topic announced in my title, since I may have to pause here and there for a few moments to perform this other (theoretical? political?) duty; but I feel I must.

Let me take as my somewhat remote point of departure the passages in Nietzsche in which he assesses Spinoza, and let me narrow the focus by excluding the many approving ones (after all, the young Nietzsche was formed in part by reading Spinoza's *Ethics*) and looking only at the judgments that seem negative. These are found essentially in *The Gay Science*, for example, in aphorisms 349 and 372:

> The wish to preserve oneself is the symptom of a condition of distress, of a limitation of the really fundamental instinct of life which aims at *the expansion of power* and, wishing for that, frequently risks and even sacrifices self-preservation. It should be considered symptomatic when some philosophers—for example Spinoza, who was consumptive—considered the instinct of self-preservation decisive.[1]

> Looking at these figures, even Spinoza, don't you have a sense of something profoundly enigmatic and uncanny? Don't you notice the spectacle that unrolls before you, how they become *ever paler*—how desensualization is interpreted more and more ideally? Don't you sense a long-concealed vampire in the background who begins with the senses and in the end is left with, and leaves, mere bones, mere clatter? I mean categories, formulas, *words* (for, forgive me, what was left of Spinoza, *amor intellectualis dei*, is mere clatter and no

more than that: what is *amor*, what *deus*, if there is not a drop of blood in them?)[2]

And finally there is aphorism 198 from *Beyond Good and Evil*: "prudence, prudence, prudence, mixed with stupidity, stupidity, stupidity . . . [of] that laughing-no-more and weeping-no-more of Spinoza, his so naively advocated destruction of the affects through their analysis and vivisection."[3]

So we have this clump of passages where Nietzsche attacks Spinoza. What are we to make of them? They treat Spinoza as a theologian of sorts: nature acts in ways that somehow turn out to be ethical. But since, for Nietzsche, nature operates waste and destruction on herself, he rejects the very idea of preservation in nature and nature's transformation into virtue, all of it leading up to *amor intellectualis*. As Nietzsche sees it, the continuity of nature and history is interrupted by the will to power.

Let us keep this Nietzschean stance in mind, and return to it at the end in order to emphasize how strongly it appears to coincide with the reading of a certain number of commentators today, or with certain interpretative tendencies that appear to reverse by 180 degrees the reading of Spinoza that obtained around 1968.

To our main topic, then: singularity and multitude. It is not easy to define what a singularity is for Spinoza. Every time one enters the thought-world of Spinoza, one feels as though one might be toppling into a fathomless abyss, and even if one doesn't, one feels its draw nonetheless, a sort of fearful desire brushing against the mind. There have been those who have experienced the reading of the *Ethics* as something akin to contact with pre-Socratic philosophy. Be that as it may, let us approach the brink of the abyss and try to define singularity. A trail is blazed in proposition XXIV of part V of the *Ethics*: "The more we understand particular things, the more do we understand God."[4] This is an echo of the corollary of proposition XXV of part I: "Particular things are nothing but modifications [*affectiones*] of the attributes of God, or modes by which the attributes of God are expressed in a fixed and definite manner."[5] From there we may go back to part V, to the demonstration of proposition XXIX and the note to it, in which the relation between the singularity of the body and the activity of the mind is considered from the perspective of eternity: "Things are conceived by us as actual in two ways: either we conceive them as existing in relation to a given time and place, or we conceive them as contained in God and following from the necessity of the divine nature. Whatever we conceive in this second way as true or real, we conceive under the form of eternity."[6]

And again, *Ethics*, part II, proposition XLV, and the note, where the eternal and infinite essence of God is conceived as the substance of every existing and singular thing in action. And again—in this game of "geometric" cross-references that it is so difficult to qualify but that are perhaps true ontological *designs*—*Ethics*, part I, proposition XXIV, the corollary: "Hence it follows that God is not only the cause of things coming into existence, but also of their continuing in existence."[7] As we can see, singularity does not eventuate exclusively or through the ontological definition of things; it also plays in or through the definition of intuitive knowledge, knowledge of the third kind, that is:[8] intuitive knowledge of singular things is more potent than universal knowledge of the second kind.

Thus, whether we are talking in ontological terms or logical ones, singularity always exists in the same perspective as eternity. This vision of singularity embedded in eternity is an intuitive certitude that grounds the awareness that "besides men, we know of no singular thing in nature in whose mind we may rejoice, and whom we can associate with ourselves in friendship or any sort of fellowship."[9]

Singularity is consequently defined as: (1) nonindividuality, because (2) it is inserted into a common, eternal substance, (3) and yet, in this substance, on the basis of this ontological insistence there emerges something that is marked by an irreducible haecceity, by a singularity also irreducible, by a mark of eternity, and (4) it lives and transforms itself in an ethical movement, or more exactly, in an interindividual rapport. If matters stand thus, if the singularity is within the common, then what sort of representation can we have of it, not just in ontological terms but in phenomenological and political ones too, amid the multitude of other singularities?

The singularities have two ways of being in the multitude. The first is its existence qua multitude. It is the process that recomposes singularities in the multitude following the principle of utility. Once more, then, chapter XXVI from part IV of the *Ethics*: "Besides men, we know of no particular thing in nature in whose mind we may rejoice, and whom we can associate with ourselves in friendship or any sort of fellowship." It is in the rapport among the singularities that *being-multitude* comes about. There you have the given of our existence.

Yet we experience the relation between singularity and multitude not just as existential (so to speak, phenomenological) tension, but also as mutation. The singularity undergoes metamorphosis, to the extent that men are not born capable of civil life, but rather become so.[10] This metamorphosis is constructive; it is the core of the relation between singularity and the multitude. Precisely because the multitude, given its existential consistency, reaches a limit, this limit must be surpassed from the inside. To put it more starkly: the single person fears solitude: "But since fear of solitude exists in all men, because no one in solitude is strong enough to defend himself, and procure the necessaries of life, it follows that men naturally aspire to the civil state; nor can it happen that men should ever utterly dissolve it."[11]

The state of nature appears to be dominated by the emotions of fear and solitude. But the fear of solitude is something more than a simple fear: it is the desire for multitude, desire for security in the multitude, desire for the absolute in the multitude. But before this desire achieves expression, the singularities are in a strange, and in certain respects ambiguous, situation, a situation phenomenologically determined. Certainly the singularity oscillates between the fear of solitude and the comfort it finds in the bosom of the common; that oscillation opens onto a higher power. Why isn't security alone enough? Men could, in effect, very well construct a "Stateless society" within the common, that is to say, they could acknowledge their natural and mutual relationship of insecurity and conflictuality, and resolve it with a pact. We know how Spinoza frames the contract in the *Tractatus theologico-politicus*: it is the constitution of singularities as multitude in its phenomenological dimension; it is, so to speak, a (contractual) condition homologous to the "Stateless society" because it is still part of *being-multitude*.

I mentioned a moment ago that there are two ways of *being-multitude*. The first is the existence itself of the multitude, as we have seen, the rapport among the singularities who constitute the multitude following principles of utility. In this process, there are tensions and mutations. The political face of this *being-multitude* is the dimension of what we have sought to identify as the condition of an illusory "Stateless society." "Stateless"—this terms needs to be understood here in all its ambiguity, or at any rate that apparent in the *ancien régime* State: "Stateless" in the sense of "without the construction of any collective, common project, any project of existence." Now it is impossible for there to be any common existence without the development of a common *cupiditas*, without an opening-up to the *cupiditates*, without the integration of the *cupiditates* into a project of common *amor*.

The second, contrasting manner of *being-multitude* has the character of a process constitutive of the human condition, in other words, of the rapport between the singularities and the multitude. The second manner of *being-multitude* [*être-multitude*] is, in the strict sense, *making-multitude* [*faire-multitude*]. It is a material and collective process directed by the common passion. The *multitudo* here increasingly wears the aspect of a *constitutio multitudinis* [a self-constitution of the multitude]. The possibility of a Stateless society is no longer available, because it is the potency of the multitude that constructs the law—this public law customarily called the State. There we have the birth of the Republic.[12] Civil law and the Republic are the potency of the *multitudo*—and the law is democratic because it is men who have constructed it.

This is the moment at which democratic expression and active consensus replace contract, the moment at which a method grounded in the common rapport among the singularities replaces any other possible rapport between isolated individuals: the potency to produce the Republic, *the making of the multitude*, take the place of contract.

Note as well that in this passage from natural law contractualism over into ethical materialism, the rapport between the singularities and the multitude also finds resolution. There exists a symmetry between, on one hand, *being-multitude* and the fact of being stuck in the dimension of the contract, and *making-multitude* and the fact of constructing political reality, on the other. In the second case, the one of interest to us, power eventuates on the basis of a *doing*, of a common praxis. From that there flows a conception of power that is always interrupted, always open, always dual until the point where this dualism is itself resolved: that is what the life of the Republic is. "Nobody can so completely transfer to another all his right, and consequently his power, as to cease to be a human being, nor will there ever be a sovereign power that can do all it pleases."[13] So the defense of liberty can only be democratic, grounded in tolerance and at the same time on the realization of liberty.[14] It is not a matter of simple natural rights, but of a certain idea of power.

With the "social contract" out of the way, the rapport between the subject and the multitude becomes central to the constitutive process in the *Ethics* and the *Tractatus politicus*. The republican political subject is the multitudinous citizen; there will henceforth be no more distinction between the subject and the citizen; sovereignty and power are returned to the multitude and reside where the potency of the organized multitude also resides.[15] The adage that *tantum iuris quantum potentiae* [there is law to the extent that there is potency] starts to impose itself here as the key to multitude-making, because it also signifies the converse: *tantum potentiae, quantum iuris* [there is potency to the extent that there is law].

One last remark. When the relation between the singularities and the multitude draws tighter within the apparatus of the creation of law, the preceding affirmation—that is, "nor will there ever be a sovereign power that can do all it pleases"—remains true despite all. Even in the unitary constitution of the multitude for the purpose of constructing the law, in the movement that transforms the multitude of singularities into power that constitutes juridical authority and functions as interpretative source in its development—well, even in this case, the opening-up of the concept of multitude to the movement of the singularities (and vice versa) always remains fundamental. This is just one more reason why the concept of *multitudo* can never be reduced to that other concept, *people*—and I insist particularly on this crucial point. The multitude does not exist apart from the difference of the singularities and the radicality of the expression "to be man." Or apart from the rapport with a *making of the Republic*.

It is here that we start to become aware of the ontological intensity, the absolute intensity, of this constitutive process.

Of course, the multitude is not without vices:

> And what we have written will, perhaps, be received with derision by those who limit vices which are inherent in all mortals to the populace only, asserting that the mob knows no restraint, that it terrorizes others unless it is cowed itself, that the populace either serves humbly or dominates arrogantly, that it has neither truth nor judgment. But *nature is one and common to all. . . .* Haughtiness is peculiar to those exerting dominance.[16]

The reader will see that what Spinoza has to say is particularly realistic. The vices of multitudinous power—when its constituent capacity, when permanent constituent control, are stripped of potency—are actually those that characterize power of any sort. But if we consider *making-multitude* as a structural process in which singularities are related to each other in a relation that has the characteristics of eternity and that implies a divine causality, then it is possible to eliminate these problems, because to enter into relation on the basis of this rapport is to develop singularity, difference, resistance. It is to strive for *amor*, it is to realize *conatus* in the form of *cupiditas*, and perhaps more still.

The rapport between the singularities and the multitude is thus teleological, but this is a teleology that has nothing to do with theology. Here finality comes from below; it is intrinsic to praxis, to conflict, meaning to the ethical movement of *making-multitude*. The conclusion of Spinoza's *Ethics*, from the political point of view, is not the reconstruction of the organic but the construction of the common. "The good which every man who strains after virtue desires for himself, he will also desire for other men, the more so in proportion as he has a greater knowledge of God."[17] It is even clearer in definition VIII of the *Ethics*, part IV: "By virtue and potency [*potentia*] I mean the same thing; that is, virtue, to the extent it pertains to man, is man's very essence or nature, to the extent that he has the ability to effect certain things that can be understood solely by the laws of that nature."[18] When knowledge of the third sort intervenes, when intuitive science imposes itself, then the synthesis between the singularities and the multitude becomes complete, indefinite, and uninterrupted: "For, although in Part I, I showed in general terms, that all things (and consequently also the human mind) depend as to their essence and existence on God, yet that demonstration, though legitimate and placed beyond the hazard of doubt, does not affect our mind so much, as when the same conclusion is derived from the actual essence of some singular thing, which we say depends on God."[19]

Intuitive knowledge is internal to praxis and constitutes the common.[20] The process and the movement of the singularities, after having traversed the existential condition, produce themselves as the common: existence itself produces itself as the common, and produces the common as multitude. It would be impossible to assemble the singularities into the multitude, if the construction of the common were not a continuous and interdependent process. The difficulties that hamper this development are all negative determinations, absence of being, lapses or insufficiencies of the constitutive process, that is to say, of the process of the desire for liberty. The teleological apparatus discovers its condition starting from below. It eventuates as tension between poverty and love: the poverty of man who is born miserable and incapable of surviving if, at the moment of becoming a subject of sociality, he is not borne up by the solidarity of other men. But only love can extract us from this poverty—love as an ontological, collective force, something completely different from the sort of erotic egoism to which "possessive individualism" has reduced love, and from the sort of religious mysticism that pushes love toward de-singularization.

Allow me, therefore, a few remarks. In the first place: the practical preeminence of doing (a doing that reaches teleologically toward the common) is articulated on the basis of a schema that corresponds to a logical, inductive, realistic, and experimental process—the production of "common ideas." This is a necessary shift from the ontology of the singularities to that of the multiple, and this shift is constructed by praxis, even on the terrain of knowledge. Second point: on this basis, it is hard to see how a certain number of skeptical reservations that have been advanced against this practical advancement of reason can stand, as though the constitution of common being could be indifferent to the common that love determines through the generation of life—and through the political organization of life as well. If evil (or fascism) is lying in wait to seize its chance in the space that leads from *being-multitude* to *making-multitude* (whether it be the fascism of animality or humanity, or just the formal automatism of obedience); if our life is continually obliged to face up to certain regressions (and every nondemocratic political form is a regression: let us merely remark that monarchy, aristocracy, and democracy, as forms of government, are not placed by Spinoza in the classical order or the traditional cyclical sequence): well, all that is not enough to cast the movement of the multitude, or its striving toward liberty, into doubt. Unless we think that man desires not life but death—and consider that resistance is not an ethical act but an act of suicide.

We may now return to the critique that Nietzsche formulates with respect to precisely this process. Nature is waste, he says; any teleology is impossible, even if it is merely constructed by man out of his own singularity and constitutes the multitude. The reading that Nietzsche gives of Spinoza, while it is extremely sympathetic when it highlights Spinozan materialism, is conversely extremely harsh and combative when it attempts to strip Spinozan material-ism of the constitutive element that animates it.

Is the constitutive element creative potency? I am convinced that by working on this point it is possible to detect in Spinoza a slide or slippage—coherent from the logical perspective—from recognition of the constitutive character of being, to an insistence on the creative potency of singularity. Constitution and creation share an essential element that can be represented by the excess of the act, of praxis, meaning by the dimension of the constitu-tive process. I am convinced that Spinozan immanentism enjoys a formidable advantage over classic and modern materialism: it comprises a singular excess—or more exactly the production of this excess. This excess is wholly there in the rapport that binds *conatus* to *cupiditas*, and that pushes this relation toward *amor*. This materialism, which excludes not only the possibility that ontological innovation might have a transcendent mover, that is to say, a substance distinct from its modes, but also the possibil-ity that there could eventuate a transcendent form of recognition of the excess of being, that is to say, a purely gnoseological and in any case nonontological schematism—this materialism, then, possesses a genealogical, constitutive rhythm that produces the innovation of being.

To return to the thread of our argument, let us posit that in this progression of being, in this materialist teleology, these singularities that constitute the multitude can likewise recognize themselves and displace themselves. Finally, if we consider this process and the singular excesses it produces, we see clearly, once again, why the dynamic of the multitude cannot be locked into the fixity or into the formalism of the juridical, constitutional, and bourgeois concept of "the people."

I would not have dwelt so long on this aspect were it not that today I perceive a banal materialist interpretation of Spinozan naturalism (or from my perspective, its implicit liquidation) making a comeback in certain sectors. The revolution in the interpretation of Spinoza that began around 1968 seems to be meeting a brand of philosophical and political revisionism today that appears to contemplate Spinoza exclusively under the species of Spinozism. I was startled, for example, to read an article by Tom Nairn, a regular contributor to the *New Left Review*, published in May 2005 in the *London Review of Books*.[21] The whole article is structured as a polemic against Étienne Balibar and myself, and fraught with the idea (very Nietzschean if one assumes that Nietzsche views matter as waste and implosion) that those who speak of Spinoza in the way that Balibar and I speak of him are engaged in some sort of "redemption business," something spiritual or spiritualistic, a salvation movement. When materialists—for that, alas, is the mantle these authors wear—assume such positions, they seem to me to reveal that their conception of materialism is just a dismal outlook on life, and that their notion of politics is a very authoritarian one, all in all. Mainly, I have the impression that these folk are the defeated, and that by dint of licking their wounds they have forgotten the overflowing joy of *multitude-making*, the joy of the construction of the common.

And finally, what strikes me particularly in this case, and more generally with critiques of this type, is that ontological space turns into a void to be filled up rather than a plenum to be given organization and expression, and that the multitude is thus viewed as a sort of metaphysical residue or a term in logic—and not as a dynamic, conflictual, living interweave of singularities, made real only by the desire for the common and the revolutionary process. The *Res communis* is constructed by the plurality of trajectories that run through the real, by the potencies that express desires, by the values that are thus invented.

I have always conceived of Spinozism as developing to the cadence of the materialist philosophy of living labor and social activity. The multitude, in the manner in which I rediscovered it in Spinoza, serves to read this *plenum* of reality and history, which singularities construct. The interpretation that 1968 gave of Spinoza made of his thought the invention of an absolute democracy that has nothing to do with redemption—because what democracy needs is praxis.

| FOUR |

SPINOZA

A Sociology of the Affects

1. SPINOZA *VERSUS* SOCIOLOGY?

When I was thinking about how to organize my paper, a certain number of difficulties that hadn't occurred to me at the outset began to crop up. These difficulties have to do not so much with the project of linking Spinoza to sociology as with the way the sociological discipline is normally defined. For the most part, sociology poses as a *Wertfrei* science, meaning a nonevaluative science bearing on a specific object ("the social"), in the tradition running from Max Weber to Pierre Bourdieu. Alternatively, it presents itself as a positive discipline dealing with an institutional object: the tradition running from Durkheim to Goffman. So when it comes to the modern distinction—or conflict—among the faculties, sociology poses simultaneously as having made a complete break with all naturalistic theories of the social (a fortiori with the natural law tradition), and as having broken just as completely with any normative or performative theory of the *conatus* of the social that we call the political.

But these two ruptures are, from my perspective, unthinkable in Spinoza, and since that is the hypothesis I will defend, I find myself at odds with the title of my own article. Or to put it another way, if there is something in Spinoza that we could call a "sociology," it will be something both naturalistic and characteristic of the natural law tradition (meaning *ontologically* grounded), and performative and normative (meaning *ethically* grounded). So in even supposing the existence of such a thing as a Spinozan sociology, we are making a break of our own away from the prevailing self-definition of the sociological discipline as positive (or positivist), autonomous, and detached; in fact, we are forced to contemplate having to assign a whole new epistemological status to sociology.

Naturally the Spinozan stance I adopt is not, on its own, adequate to ground a reformulation of the disciplinary status of sociology. But Spinozism may nevertheless be the philosophical instrument best adapted to dealing with the situation we are living through. By that I mean that we can descry in Spinoza, in the theoretical alternatives and the resistance that he formulated against the modern figures of power, a perspective on actuality and an initiation into the desire to gain cognizance of the structures of society and power that are evolving right now. In sum, in the postmodern epoch, may we not recognize in the Spinozan anomaly—some might even add: in the antimodernity of the Spinozan concepts of the political and democracy—an anticipation of the future?

So back to Spinoza. First problem: what results does an analysis of the social indexed purely to the Spinozan physics of the *conatus* yield? It yields results that immediately contradict any linear and positive logic produced by sociological associationism, even when the latter presents itself in the form of an analytic of interindividual relations.

The *conatus* implies a range of things. First: an effort to persevere in one's being (to exist, that is), to preserve and expand one's own being. But secondly, this effort is expended as a function of an essential telos that is both the base and the source of value. On this point, allow me two substantial quotations from the demonstration (or proof) and scholium (or note) to proposition LVII from part III of the *Ethics* ("Any emotion of any given individual differs from the emotion of another individual to the exact degree that the essence of the one individual differs from the essence of the other"):

All emotions are attributable to desire, pleasure, or pain, as their definitions given above show. But desire is each man's nature or essence; therefore desire in each individual differs from desire in every other to the degree that each one's nature or essence differs from the nature or essence of every other. Pleasure and pain for their part are passions, whereby each man's potency [*potentia*] or endeavor [*conatus*] to persist in his being is increased or diminished, helped or hindered. But by the endeavor to persist in its being, in so far as it concerns both the mind and the body, we understand appetite and desire; therefore pleasure and pain is just desire or appetite itself, to the extent that by external causes it is increased or diminished, helped or hindered, in other words it is the very nature of every man. Wherefore the pleasure and pain of one man also differ from the pleasure and pain of another man to the degree that the nature or essence of the one differs from the essence of the other, and consequently any emotion of any individual differs from the emotion of any other to the degree . . . and so on.[1]

Hence it follows that the emotions of the animals which are called irrational (for after learning the origin of mind we cannot doubt that brutes feel) differ from man's emotions to the exact degree that their nature differs from human nature. Horse and man are alike driven by the urge to procreate; but the desire of the former is equine, the desire of the latter is human. So also the urges and appetites of insects, fish, and birds must be different in each case. Thus, although each individual lives content and rejoices in that nature by which he is what he is, yet the life wherein each is content and rejoices is nothing else but the idea or soul (*anima*) of the said individual, and hence the joy of one differs from the joy of another by nature, to the exact degree that the essence of one differs from the essence of another. A corollary of proposition LVII, I note in passing, is that there is a wide difference between the joy that draws a drunkard, say, and the joy relished by a philosopher.[2]

One might append a further scholium to the effect that if an attempt were made to construct a linear sociology of the *conatus* within an individualistic framework, the result would be a drunkard's sociology. Because it is not so much interrelationship as such that qualifies the tissue of social relations as the *essential nature* of these relations, the *ontological impulse* that animates them, and also—besides, but simultaneously—the *resistance* with which this essential nature opposes or directs itself toward the highest level of knowledge, that of the philosopher. For this level is also a level of social recomposition and constitution. Hence the remoteness of Spinoza from the sociology of the moderns could scarcely be greater.

It is not my intention here to quibble with all the attempts hitherto made to define a Spinozan sociology (of which there are more than a few): I wish only to highlight the impossibility of constructing a Spinozan sociology based on a static conception of *conatus*.

A static definition of *conatus* would be a more Hobbesian definition of *conatus*—the goal toward which all modern individualism is trying to steer us. It would necessarily be a paving of the way for a dialectical shift to another, normative level somewhere above and beyond society—a dialectical shift to power and the State. This Spinoza excludes. Indeed, he not only excludes it; it strikes him as repugnant, because this is the same process that leads to superstition.

And even if we resist the Hobbesian theory of *conatus* and consider Spinozan *conatus* as a generous and donative opening ("munificent," an affirmation of *munus*, or "gift"), whatever might be the other difficulties this approach would create in the reading of Spinoza's text—even in this case, we would not succeed in resolving this natural and ethical tension that *conatus* reveals and *cupiditas* orients. Even in this case, we would immediately be obliged to a further artificial operation consisting of introducing transcendence, in other words, a dialectical operation. For Spinozan *conatus*—and here lies its paradox—is never reducible to the generous figure of the gift. In the gift, that which is given away has necessarily been acquired somewhere else; whereas for *conatus*, the gift is a never-failing potency.

2. *CUPIDITAS* AND BIOPOLITICS

Second problem: is it possible to construct a Spinozan sociology that disrupts any linear or positive logic of individual interrelations? Past all doubt, it is. This possibility is based on the continuity of the processes of *conatus*, of *affectus/cupiditas*, but also, as Spinoza never fails to insist, of *amor*. Let us take note: continuity in Spinoza is never a linearity, but on the contrary a transition, an imagination, the internal and constitutive development of *cupiditas*. In the *Ethics*, part III, we read this "Definition of the Emotions":

I. Desire [*Cupiditas*] is the very essence of man, in so far as it is conceived, as determined to a particular activity by some given modification of itself. Explanation: . . . By the term desire, then, I here mean all man's endeavours, impulses, appetites, and volitions, which vary according to each man's disposition, and are, therefore, often so opposed one to another that a man is drawn in different directions, and knows not where to turn.

II. Pleasure is the transition of a man from a less to a greater perfection.

III. Pain is the transition of a man from a greater to a less perfection. Explanation: I say transition. For pleasure is not perfection itself. For, if man were born with the perfection to which he passes, he would possess the same, without the emotion of pleasure. This appears more clearly from the consideration of the contrary emotion, pain. No one can deny, that pain consists in the transition to a lesser perfection, and not in the lesser perfection itself: for a man cannot be pained, in so far as he partakes of perfection of any degree. Neither can we say, that pain consists in the absence of a greater perfection. For absence is nothing, whereas the emotion of pain is an activity, which can only be the activity of transition to a lesser perfection—in other words, it is an activity whereby a man's power of action is lessened or constrained. I omit the definitions of merriment, stimulation, melancholy, and grief, because they pertain primarily to the body, and are merely species of pleasure or pain.[3]

Here *cupiditas* is defined as totality: "all man's endeavours, impulses, appetites, and volitions," says Spinoza, including conscience and appetite. And this cupidity immediately undergoes a process of transition, of movement toward greater or lesser perfection, in a process of singular imagination of the future that displaces *cupiditas* from a given level of composition to another, which is superior to it. And thus, from threshold to threshold—dispersing any interrelational physics of the social through the immanent constitutive character of the development of *cupiditas*. This transition, this movement, is not interrrelational but constitutive.

This theme is of course developed, and brought to maturity, at the beginning of part V of the *Ethics*. It goes like this: no individualistic sociology can help us to comprehend the social. But an interindividual sociology cannot do so either, as long as it is defined by the dialectic of life or of jealousy, of attraction or repulsion. The sole key of a social process is nourished by *Love*.

Let us reread, in this regard, the note to proposition XX of the *Ethics*, part V, dedicated to Love toward God (*Amor erga Deum*):

We can in the same way show, that there is no emotion directly contrary to this love, whereby this love can be destroyed. Therefore we may conclude that this love towards God is the most constant of all the emotions, and that, to the extent that it pertains to the body, it cannot be destroyed, unless the body be destroyed also. As to its nature, in so far as it pertains to the mind alone, we shall presently inquire.

I have now reviewed all the remedies against the emotions, or all that the mind, considered in itself alone, can do against them. Whence it appears that the mind's power over the emotions consists:

I. In actual knowledge of the emotions.

II. In the fact that it separates the emotions from the thought of an external cause, which we conceive confusedly.

III. In the fact, that, in respect to time, the emotions referred to things, which we distinctly understand, surpass those referred to what we conceive in a confused and fragmentary manner.

IV. In the multitude of causes whereby those modifications are fostered, which have regard to the common properties of things or to God.

V. Lastly, in the order wherein the mind can arrange and associate, one with another, its own emotions.

But, in order that this power of the mind over the emotions may be better understood, it should be especially observed that the emotions are called by us strong, when we compare the emotion of one man with the emotion of another, and see that one man is more troubled than another by the same emotion; or when we are comparing the various emotions of the same man one with another, and find that he is more affected or stirred by one emotion than by another. For the strength of every emotion is defined by a comparison of our own potency with the potency of an external cause. But the potency of the mind is defined solely by knowledge, and its impotency or passion is defined solely by the privation of knowledge—that is, it is assessed by that through which ideas are described as inadequate. From this it follows, that that mind suffers most [or "undergoes the most passion," *id maxime pati*] whose greatest part is made up of inadequate ideas, so that it may be characterized more readily by what it suffers than by its activities: on the other hand, that mind is most active, whose greatest part is made up of adequate ideas, so that, although it may contain as many inadequate ideas as the former mind, it may yet be more easily characterized by ideas attributable to human virtue, than by ideas which tell of human infirmity.

Again, it must be observed, that spiritual ill-health and misfortunes can generally be traced to excessive love for something which is subject to many variations, and which we can never become masters of. For no one is solicitous or anxious about anything, unless he loves it; neither do wrongs, suspicions, enmities, etc. arise, except out of love toward things whereof no one can be really master.

We may thus readily conceive the power which clear and distinct knowledge, and especially that third kind of knowledge, founded on the actual knowledge of God, possesses over the emotions: if it does not absolutely destroy them, in so far as they are passions, at any rate, it causes them to occupy a very small part of the mind. Further, it begets a love towards a thing immutable and eternal, whereof we may really enter into possession, which on that account cannot be defiled with those faults which are inherent in ordinary love, but may grow from strength to strength, and may engross the greater part of the mind, and deeply penetrate it.

And now I have finished with all that concerns this present life: for, as I said in the beginning of this note, I have briefly described all the remedies against the emotions. And this everyone may readily see for himself, if he has attended to what is advanced in the present note, and also to the definitions of the mind and its emotions, and, lastly, to propositions I and III of part III. It is now, therefore, time to pass on to those matters, which pertain to the duration of the mind, without relation to the body.[4]

To comprehend this continuity between nature and virtue, which is progressive, organized as a function of an immanent telos, which knows no condition of necessity and is based solely on liberty, we may turn to the reading of Spinoza proposed by Gilles Deleuze. His insistence on immanence and the univocity of being constitutes a fundamental terrain of interpretation. But that is not enough.

To go further—not just further than this Deleuzian reading, but more generally further than the interpretations proposed by the generation of Matheron, Macherey, Balibar, and (bringing up the rear) Negri—we must follow the reading Pierre-François Moreau proposes, for example, or those of a whole new generation of researchers whose device appears to be: "to be in the experience of Spinoza," to be in an ontological context from the outset, in the experiential and hopeful continuity of a constitutive perspective.

To reconstruct, or better to rediscover, a Spinoza corresponding to the spirit of postmodernity, to understand and realize the alternative to the modern that he offers us (and, for present purposes, to apply this alternative to the modern conception of sociology), it is necessary to place ourselves on a terrain I will take the liberty of calling "biopolitical." So we must reread the ontological condition as a biopolitical experience.

Here I must make a slight but necessary detour in order to define the notion of "biopolitics," and understand how it can be linked to the interpretation of Spinoza. When one speaks of biopolitics, one understands (faced with an immediately comprehensible image of biopower as sovereign power that invests life) the vital articulation of the *cupiditates*, their capacity (in the constitutive interrelation that is theirs) to traverse the modes of life and consequently determine the active intersection of the polis and life. This intersection presents itself continually as a resistance, as a consistence, against the pretentions of power. It is a collective constituent potency that runs up against the obstacles of superstition, of unfreedom, and of power.

I am absolutely convinced that certain themes of late-modern sociological and economic thought, whether they actually refer to Spinoza or not, have arisen within this horizon—from Simmel to Becker, from Bourdieu to the theoreticians of productive externality. And I am equally convinced that a whole series of philosophers interested in the problem of technology (and its power of transformation, that is, of collective praxis), from Mondolfo to Simondon, from Althusser to Macherey—to cite only the most obvious names—have appreciated the potency of Spinoza's thought when it came to dissolving the fetishism of the capitalism of accumulation and development.

Support for this view can easily be found in current discussions of the relations between Spinoza and the social sciences. Nevertheless, it seems to me that we need to drag all these analytic tools back into the biopolitical context, in other words, to supply the critical dimension with a subjective substrate. Only thus can we show ourselves to be friends of *cupiditas*.

3. FROM *CUPIDITAS* TO *AMOR*

Let us close that parenthesis and return to the thread of our discourse. The unique figure of sociological analysis implicit in the philosophy of Spinoza may finally be revealed. This figure goes not simply against the grain of any simplistic physics of *conatus*, meaning far beyond any conception of individual interrelations; it presents itself as a movement entirely aimed at *the construction of the common*. By that I mean that natural law doctrine, in its individualistic dimension, is eliminated through the process of *conatus*, that it undergoes metamorphosis through an analysis of the sentiments that becomes increasingly constituent, and that it withers to nothing through the definition of a common tissue of the social, and of collective action—a tissue sustained by love. In sum: the individualistic genesis of society as described by natural law doctrine is here transformed into a performative or normative theory of the social and the political, into an effective construction of the common.

This means that when the individualistic tissue is sloughed off—and the whole Spinozan physics tends toward that—when the analysis defines the social as a constellation of singularities, then *conatus*, *appetitus*, and *cupiditas* (in a gradual arc of social constitution) definitively assume the common as ever-renewed basis and telos ever more efficaciously constructed. Between the physics and the ethics of the sentiments, the common determines the constituent motor of the ontological process.

It is probably not necessary here to read the specific passages from the *Ethics*, since matters in this respect are extremely clear.[5] We are in the presence of an ontological continuity of the world based on articulations of the social that are also its constitutive moments.

But modern sociologists, who view things from within a horizon of individualism, have the illusion that they can avoid this discontinuous continuity that defines the singularities in the common. They quite rightly reject the crass positivism of the American schools, yet that is not enough. There is a further step they must take to get to the correct dimension we have just described, that is, to keep the processes of resistance and constitution from being crushed or attenuated through interrelationism.

In Spinoza the continuity of the process of *cupiditas* enhances the discontinuity of the constitutive process of the real. It accentuates the ontological consistency of the social: because Spinoza simply proposes, to all who want to be in the social, to really be there. The only possible point of view of a Spinozan sociology is that of *cupiditas* acting in the social, in the immanence of being, in the necessary construction of the common. Does that mean it is possible to define the Spinozan approach to sociology as genealogical, and the figure of the Spinozan sociologist as an analyst of the genealogy of social being? In sum: as the agent of a construction of social being that is at the same time productive, resolutive, and capable of ruptures, potent in its capacity to define material relations and the intervention of knowledge in the social? In pushing the question toward a terrain of improper relationships, I am almost prepared to ask: is a Foucauldian definition of the sociological thought of Spinoza possible?

My answer would be: paradoxically, yes. I insist, of course, on the improper character of this relationship between the two thinkers. Foucault did not know Spinoza well, unless Spinoza belongs among the authors with whom he claimed he was familiar but whom he did not cite. To simplify the problem, let us add that in the entire oeuvre of Foucault the name of Spinoza only crops up half a dozen times, generally in the course of summaries by Foucault of what he had read in the work of other philosophers. Despite that, I believe that Foucault may have something to contribute to the construction of a hypothetical Spinozan sociology, by which I mean that between the *Ethics* of Spinoza and in the work of the late Foucault one discovers an impressive number of analogies.

When the philosopher Laurent Bove speaks of a "strategy of *conatus*" that, through impulses of resistance, constructs the social, and when some sociological critics (I am thinking particularly of the works of Pascal Nicolas-Le Strat) take from Foucault a methodology of singular resistance as the basis of social knowledge, they both deconstruct and recompose a genealogy of the passions within the long and fatiguing process of sociological *Verstehen*. I am reminded of the handful of radical breaks that the discipline of sociological individualism experienced in the twentieth century, at the hands of Georg Simmel, epigone of the modern, and of Michel de Certeau, the remarkable historian who anticipated an open and positive postmodernity. Simmel and Certeau, Bove and Nicolas-Le Strat, have highlighted anew the Spinozan paradigm. Better: they have interpreted a "Spinozan moment" in the reconstruction of an epistemology constitutive of the real.

They do not, of course, receive a particularly warm welcome from the sociological discipline. I think, for example, of an intervention by the sociologist Jean-Louis Fabiani at a recent colloquy on Foucault, in which he examines the question of whether or not Foucault's *The Archeology of Knowledge* can be recuperated within historical sociology (and thus within sociology in general). He regards the hypothesis as highly improbable overall. If one analyzes Foucault's positions with regard to classical sociology (Durkheim and Weber), it is easy to show that his own program is situated at a different level than that of the social sciences. But that is an important fact to recognize, for those of us who stand on firm Spinozan terrain. Foucault is just as remote from the sociology of individualism and *Wertfrei* methods as Spinoza, because participation in the construction of the social, in a free and democratic construction, is something foreign to classic and professional sociology. Does that act of recognition not justify the tentative hypothesis of an analogy or link between Spinoza and Foucault, since both attempted to destroy individualism and methodological collectivism in sociology? I naturally leave the question open.

Let us wrap things up. The route from associative *conatus* to constitutive *amor* may be a long one, but the journey is still necessary—Spinoza *dixit*—from the perspective of epistemology, as much as from that of ontology. It is on the basis of a strategy of *amor* that a Spinozan sociology, normative and linked to natural law, ontological and performative, can be constructed.

Amor. I sometimes find myself writing or speaking about "love" in the context of sociological discourse. The reward this earns me is generally irony and sarcasm. How difficult it is to wrench love away from the psychological vanity of romanticism, or the ferocious utopia of mysticism! For that in reality is how love has been interpreted (or evaded) by modernity. For me, on the contrary, love as defined by Spinoza introduces us to the rational and constructive rapport between constituent ontological potency and the collective action of the singularities. In this sense, a possible Spinozan sociology would constitute a sort of laboratory working against and beyond the modern, against and beyond possessive individualism. It would embrace *amor* as a subversive force, showing society as the constitution of the common, as the inter-secting of the rationality and desire of singularities, as the trajectory of common liberty.

In Spinoza, there is consequently something even more advanced and more potent than all that we have attempted to sketch hitherto. This something is his absolutely materialist—that is to say, biopolitical—consciousness. Here we have a synonymy that can be utilized today to express immanence in a radical manner. Materialist and biopolitical consciousness, then, of the fact that the social is political, of the fact that interindividual relations are, through the play of singularities, immediately reprised in the common. The production of institutions, which finds its dynamic origin in the potency of *cupiditas*, in that of desire, passes through the singularities to construct the common. The ever-more-effective construction of institutional relations is the consequence of an ever-fuller production of self. Spinozan pantheism—one wonders why nobody, not even the most confessional of philosophers, speaks of it anymore today?—is the recognition of the force of man in the production of the true through the common exercise of love. Democracy is an act of love.

If the sociology of Spinoza is the analysis of this movement, then the politics that springs from sociological research can only be the collective management of the common.

NOTES

INTRODUCTION: SPINOZA AND US

1. Antonio Negri, *L'Anomalie sauvage: Puissance et pouvoir chez Spinoza*, trans. F. Matheron (1982; Paris: Editions Amsterdam, 2006); Negri, *The Savage Anomaly: The Power of Spinoza's Metaphysics and Politics*, trans. Michael Hardt (Minneapolis: University of Minnesota Press, 1991). The Italian original was published in 1981.
2. Cf. Tom Nairn, "Make for the Boondocks," *London Review of Books*, 5 May 2005.
3. Cf. Paolo Cristofolini, "Piccolo lessico ragionato," appendix to *Tractatus politicus/trattato politico*, by Baruch Spinoza (Pisa: ETS, 1999).
4. Étienne Balibar, *Spinoza et la politique* (Paris: PUF, 1985); Manfred Walther, "Institution, Imagination, und Freiheit bei Spinoza: Eine kritische

Theorie politischer Institutionen," in *Politische Institutionen im gesell-
schaftlichen Umbruch: Ideengeschichtliche Beiträge zur Theorie politischer
Institutionen*, ed. Gerhard Göhler, Kurt Lenk, Herfried Münkler, and
Manfred Walther (Opladen: Westdeutscher Verlag, 1990), pp. 246–275;
Moira Gatens, *Imaginary Bodies: Ethics, Power, and Corporeality* (London:
Routledge, 1995).

5. Alexandre Matheron, *Individu et communauté chez Spinoza* (Paris: Minuit, 1969).

6. Gilles Deleuze, *Spinoza et le problème de l'expression* (Paris: Minuit, 1968);
Deleuze, *Expressionism in Philosophy: Spinoza*, trans. Martin Joughin
(New York: Zone Books, 1992).

7. Gilles Deleuze, "L'immanence: une vie . . . ," in *Philosophie*, no. 47 (Paris:
Minuit, 1995).

8. Cf. Antonio Negri, *Spinoza subversif: Variations (in)actuelles*, trans. M.
Raiola and F. Matheron (Paris: Kimé, 1994); Negri, *Subversive Spinoza:
(Un)contemporary Variations*, ed. Timothy S. Murphy, trans. Timothy S.
Murphy, Michael Hardt, Ted Stolze, and Charles T. Wolfe (Manchester:
Manchester University Press, 2004).

9. Laurent Bove, *La strategie du conatus* (Paris: Vrin, 1996).

10. Filippo Del Lucchese, *Tumultes et indignation: Conflit, droit, et multitude
chez Machiavel et Spinoza*, trans. P. Pasquini (Paris: Amsterdam, 2009).

11. Gilles Deleuze, *Spinoza: Philosophie practique* (Paris: Minuit, 1981);
Deleuze, *Spinoza: Practical Philosophy*, trans. Robert Hurley (San Francisco: City Lights, 2001).

12. Spinoza, *Ethics*, part IV, prop. LXI.

13. Spinoza, *Ethics*, part IV, prop. LXXXIII.

14. V. Morfino and F. Piro, eds., *Spinoza: resistenza e conflitto*, in *Quaderni
materialisti* no. 5 (Milan: Ghibli, 2006). [Translated into English from the
French translation of the Italian original by Judith Revel. WM]

15. Filippo Del Lucchese, "Sedizione e modernita: La divisione come politica
e il conflitto come libertà in Machiavelli e Spinoza," in Morfino and Piro,
Spinoza: resistenza e conflitto, p. 10. [Translated into English from the
French translation of the Italian original by Judith Revel. WM]

16. Del Lucchese, "Sedizione e modernita," p. 13.

17. Cf. Antonio Negri, "Note sulla storia del politico in Tronti," appendix 3 to *L'Anomalia selvaggia* (Milan: Feltrinelli, 1981), pp. 288–292; and the translation in Negri, *The Savage Anomaly*.

18. Del Lucchese, "Sedizione e modernita," p. 27. [Translated into English from the French translation of the Italian original by Judith Revel. WM]

19. Ibid. p. 31. Cf. Bove, *La strategie du conatus*, and more generally Michael Hardt and Antonio Negri, *Multitude: War and Democracy in the Age of Empire* (New York: Penguin, 2004); and Hardt and Negri, *Commonwealth* (Cambridge, Mass.: Harvard University Press, 2009).

20. Cf. Giorgio Agamben, *The Time That Remains: A Commentary on the Letter to the Romans*, trans. Patricia Dailey (Stanford: Stanford University Press 2005), first published in Italian and French in 2000; Paolo Virno, "Il cosìdetto 'male' e la critica dello Stato," *Forme di vita* 4 (2005): 9–36.

21. Antonio Negri, *Descartes politico o della ragionevole ideologia* (1970; Rome: Manifestolibri, 2007); Negri, *Political Descartes: Reason, Ideology and the Bourgeois Project*, trans. Matteo Mandarini and Alberto Toscano (London: Verso, 2007); in the latter, see the "Postface to the English Edition," pp. 317–338.

22. Augusto Illuminati, "Sul principio di obbligazione," in Morfino and Piro, *Spinoza: resistenza e conflitto*, p. 36. [Translated into English from the French translation of the Italian original by Judith Revel. WM]

23. François Zourabichvili, "L'enigma della 'moltitudine libera,'" in Morfino and Piro, *Spinoza, resistenza e conflitto*, p. 108. [Translated into English from the French translation of the Italian original by Judith Revel. WM]

24. Cf. Crawford Brough Macpherson, *The Political Theory of Possessive Individualism: Hobbes to Locke* (Oxford: Oxford University Press, 1962); John Rawls, *Lectures on the History of Political Philosophy* (Cambridge, Mass.: Harvard University Press, 2007).

25. Margaret C. Jacob, *The Radical Enlightenment: Pantheists, Freemasons, and Republicans* (London-Boston: Allen and Unwin, 1981; second edition: Morristown: The Temple Publishers, 2003).

26. Jonathan I. Israel, *Radical Enlightenment: Philosophy and the Making of Modernity, 1650–1750* (New York: Oxford University Press, 2001).

27. Cf. Catherine Secrétan, Tristan Dagron, and Laurent Bove, eds., *Qu'est-ce que les Lumières "radicales"?* (Paris: Amsterdam, 2007).

28. Antoine Lilti, "Comment écrit-on l'histoire intellectuelle des Lumières? Spinozisme, radicalisme et philosophie," in *Annales HSS* (64th year, no. 1), 2009, pp. 171–206.

29. Cf. Negri, "Postface to the English Edition," in *Political Descartes*.

30. Louis Althusser, "L'unique tradition matérialiste," *Lignes* 18 (1993): 71–119.

31. See Alain Badiou, *Théorie du sujet* (Paris: Le Seuil, 1982); Badiou, *Deleuze* (Paris: Hachette, 1997); Badiou, *Court traité d'ontologie transitoire* (Paris: Le Seuil, 1998). English translations: Badiou, *Theory of the Subject*, trans. Bruno Bosteels (New York: Continuum, 2009); Badiou, *Deleuze: The Clamor of Being*, trans. Louise Burchill (Minneapolis: University of Minnesota Press, 2000); Badiou, *Briefings on Existence: A Short Treatise on Transitory Ontology*, trans. Norman Madarasz (Albany: SUNY Press, 2006).

32. Emanuele Severino, "Spinoza, Dio, e il Nulla," *Corriere della Sera*, 30 June 2007.

33. Spinoza, *Ethics*, part IV, prop. LXVII.

34. Spinoza, *Ethics*, part II, prop. XLIII, note.

35. Cf. Étienne Balibar, "Potentia multitudinis, quae una veluti mente ducitur," in *Ethik, Recht, und Politik bei Spinoza*, ed. Marcel Senn and Manfred Walther (Zurich: Schulthess, 2001), pp. 105–137.

36. See, e.g., Massimo Cacciari, *Krisis* (Milan: Feltrinelli, 1976).

37. Cf. Pierre-François Moreau, *Spinoza: L'expérience et l'éternité* (Paris: PUF, 1994), and the works of Laurent Bove cited above.

38. I think that, each in his own way, both Giorgio Agamben in his *Homo Sacer: Sovereign Power and Bare Life* and Roberto Esposito in his *Bìos: Biopolitics and Philosophy* manifestly represent the continuation of this Frankfurt lineage. Agamben, *Homo Sacer: Sovereign Power and Bare Life*, trans. Daniel Heller-Roazen (Stanford: Stanford University Press, 1998), first published in Italian in 1995; Roberto Esposito, *Bìos: Biopolitics and Philosophy*, trans. Timothy Campbell (Minneapolis: University of Minnesota Press, 2008), first published in Italian in 2004.

39. Cf. Michel Foucault, *Dits et Écrits* (Paris: Gallimard, 1994), esp. vols. 3 and 4, as well as the courses given at the Collège de France starting in the late 1970s.

40. Alexandre Matheron, *Le Christ et le salut des Ignorants chez Spinoza* (Paris: Éditions Aubier-Montaigne, 1971).

41. Chantal Jacquet, *Sub specie aeternitatis: Étude des concepts de temps, durée et éternité chez Spinoza* (Paris: Kimé, 1997); and more recently, Jacquet, *Les Expressions de la puissance d'agir chez Spinoza* (Paris: Presses de la Sorbonne, 2005).

42. Jacques Rancière, *Disagreement: Politics and Philosophy*, trans. Julie Rose (Minneapolis: University of Minnesota Press, 1999). First published in French in 1995.

43. Étienne Balibar, "Spinoza: la crainte des masses," in *Spinoza nel 350° anniversario dalla nascita*, ed. Emilia Giancotti (Naples: Bibliopolis, 1985), pp. 293–320.

1. SPINOZA: A HERESY OF IMMANENCE
AND OF DEMOCRACY

1. Cf. Negri, *Political Descartes: Reason, Ideology, and the Bourgeois Project*, trans. Matteo Mandarini and Alberto Toscano (London: Verso, 2007).

2. Cf. Negri, "Postface to the English Edition," in *Political Descartes*.

3. Cf. Negri, *The Savage Anomaly: The Power of Spinoza's Metaphysics and Politics*, trans. Michael Hardt (Minneapolis: University of Minnesota Press, 1991).

4. I take the liberty of referring on this point to some writings of my own, including chapter 2 in this volume, and "Giorgio Agamben: The Discreet Taste of the Dialectic," in *Giorgio Agamben: Sovereignty and Life*, ed. Matthew Calarco and Steven DeCaroli (Stanford: Stanford University Press, 2007).

5. Maurice Merleau-Ponty, *Signes* (Paris: Gallimard, 1960); Merleau-Ponty, *Signs*, trans. Richard McCleary (Evanston, Ill.: Northwestern University Press, 1964).

6. Spinoza, *Ethics*, part IV, prop. LXI.
7. Negri, *Kairòs, Alma Venus, multitude*, trans. Judith Revel (Paris: Calmann-Lévy, 2001).
8. Gilles Deleuze, "L'immanence: une vie . . . ," in *Philosophie*, no. 47 (Paris: Minuit, 1995).
9. Spinoza, *Ethics*, part IV, prop. LXXIII.

2. POTENCY AND ONTOLOGY: HEIDEGGER OR SPINOZA

1. Martin Heidegger, *Sein und Zeit* (cited by 1927 pagination), p. 1. English translation from Heidegger, *Being and Time*, trans. Joan Stambaugh (Albany: SUNY Press, 1996), which supplies the 1927 pagination in the margins.
2. Heidegger, *Sein und Zeit*, pp. 14–15, Stambaugh translation.
3. Heidegger, *Sein und Zeit*, pp. 435–436, Stambaugh translation.
4. Heidegger, *Sein und Zeit*, p. 227, Stambaugh translation.
5. Heidegger, *Sein und Zeit*, p. 228, Stambaugh translation.
6. Spinoza, *Ethics*, part V, prop. XXIX.
7. Spinoza, *Ethics*, part V, prop. XXX.
8. Spinoza, *Ethics*, part V, prop. XXXII, corollary.
9. Spinoza, *Ethics*, part V, prop. XXXIII, note.
10. Spinoza, *Ethics*, part V, prop. XXXIV, note.
11. Spinoza, *Ethics*, part V, prop. XXXVI, proof.
12. Spinoza, *Ethics*, part V, prop. XXXVI, note.
13. Spinoza, *Ethics*, part V, prop. XL.

3. MULTITUDE AND SINGULARITY IN THE DEVELOPMENT OF THE POLITICAL THOUGHT OF SPINOZA

1. Friedrich Nietzsche, *The Gay Science*, trans. Walter Kaufmann (New York: Vintage Books, 1974), aphorism 349 (excerpt).

2. Nietzsche, *The Gay Science*, aphorism 372 (excerpt).
3. Friedrich Nietzsche, *Beyond Good and Evil*, in *Basic Writings of Nietzsche*, trans. Walter Kaufmann (New York: Modern Library, 1968), aphorism 198 (excerpt).
4. Spinoza, *Ethics*, part V, prop. XXIV.
5. Spinoza, *Ethics*, part I, prop. XXV, corollary.
6. Spinoza, *Ethics*, part V, prop. XXIX, note.
7. Spinoza, *Ethics*, part I, prop. XXIV, corollary.
8. Spinoza, *Ethics*, part V, prop. XXXVI, note; and Spinoza, *Ethics*, part V, prop. XL, note.
9. Spinoza, *Ethics*, part IV, appendix, chap. XXVI.
10. "For men are not born citizens, they become so." Spinoza, *Tractatus politicus*, chap. 5, para. 2.
11. Spinoza, *Tractatus politicus*, chap. 6, para. 1.
12. "This right [*ius*], which is determined by the potency [*potentia*] of the multitude, is generally called sovereignty [*imperium*]. And he who by common consent has charge of affairs of state [*curam Reipublicae*], such as issuing, interpreting, and abrogating laws [*iura*], fortifying cities, and decreeing war and peace, holds it absolutely." Spinoza, *Tractatus politicus*, chap. 2, para. 17.
13. Baruch Spinoza, *Tractatus theologico-politicus*, trans. Samuel Shirley (Leiden: Brill, 1991), chap. 17, p. 250.
14. Spinoza, *Tractatus theologico-politicus*, chap. 17.
15. Spinoza, *Tractatus politicus*, chap. 3, section 9.
16. Spinoza, *Tractatus politicus*, chap. 7, para. 27.
17. Spinoza, *Ethics*, part IV, prop. XXXVII.
18. Spinoza, *Ethics*, part IV, def. VIII.
19. Spinoza, *Ethics*, part V, prop. XXXVI, note.
20. Spinoza, *Ethics*, part II, prop. XL, note II.
21. Tom Nairn, "Make for the Boondocks," *London Review of Books*, 5 May 2005.

4. SPINOZA: A SOCIOLOGY OF THE AFFECTS

1. Spinoza, *Ethics*, part III, prop. LVII, proof.

2. Spinoza, *Ethics*, part III, prop. LVII, note.
3. Spinoza, *Ethics*, part III, "Definitions of the Emotions" and "Explanations."
4. Spinoza, *Ethics*, part V, prop. XX, note. On this subject, see also Spinoza, *Ethics*, part V, axiom II; prop. IV, note; and props. XIV–XX.
5. I will indicate just one possible sequence of readings out of many to enable readers to locate this common horizon that the passions live and fix in a contradictory manner: Spinoza, *Ethics*, part II, props. XXXVII–XXXIX; Spinoza, *Ethics*, part III, props. XXXV–XL; Spinoza, *Ethics*, part V, note to proposition X.

BIBLIOGRAPHY

Agamben, Giorgio. *Homo Sacer: Sovereign Power and Bare Life*. Translated by Daniel Heller-Roazen. Stanford: Stanford University Press, 1998. First published in Italian in 1995.

——. *The Time That Remains: A Commentary on the Letter to the Romans*. Translated by Patricia Dailey. Stanford: Stanford University Press, 2005. First published in Italian and French in 2000.

Althusser, Louis. "L'unique tradition matérialiste." *Lignes* 18 (1993): 71–119.

Badiou, Alain. *Court traité d'ontologie transitoire*. Paris: Le Seuil, 1998. English Translation: *Briefings on Existence: A Short Treatise on Transitory Ontology*. Translated by Norman Madarasz. Albany: SUNY Press, 2006.

——. *Deleuze*. Paris: Hachette, 1997. English Translation: *Deleuze: The Clamor of Being*. Translated by Louise Burchill. Minneapolis: University of Minnesota Press, 2000.

——. *Théorie du sujet*. Paris: Le Seuil, 1982. English Translation: *Theory of the Subject*. Translated by Bruno Bosteels. New York: Continuum, 2009.

Balibar, Étienne. "Potentia multitudinis, quae una veluti mente ducitur." In *Ethik, Recht, und Politik bei Spinoza*, edited by Marcel Senn and Manfred Walther, pp. 105–137. Zurich: Schulthess, 2001.

——. *Spinoza et la politique*. Paris: PUF, 1985.

——. "Spinoza: La crainte des masses." In *Spinoza nel 350° anniversario dalla nascita*, edited by Emilia Giancotti, pp. 293–320. Naples: Bibliopolis, 1985.

Bove, Laurent. *La strategie du conatus*. Paris: Vrin, 1996.

Cacciari, Massimo. *Krisis*. Milan: Feltrinelli, 1976.

Cristofolini, Paolo. "Piccolo lessico ragionato." Appendix to *Tractatus politicus/trattato politico*, by Baruch Spinoza. Pisa: ETS, 1999.

Deleuze, Gilles. "L'immanence: une vie . . . ," in *Philosophie*, no. 47. Paris: Minuit, 1995.

——. *Spinoza et le problème de l'expression*. Paris: Minuit, 1968. English translation: *Expressionism in Philosophy: Spinoza*. Translated by Martin Joughin. New York: Zone Books, 1992.

——. *Spinoza: Philosophie practique*. Paris: Minuit, 1981. English translation: *Spinoza: Practical Philosophy*. Translated by Robert Hurley. San Francisco: City Lights, 2001.

Del Lucchese, Filippo. "Sedizione e modernita: La divisione come politica e il conflitto come libertà in Machiavelli e Spinoza." In Morfino and Piro, *Spinoza, resistenza e conflitto*, p. 10.

——. *Tumultes et indignation: Conflit, droit, et multitude chez Machiavel et Spinoza*. Translated by P. Pasquini. Paris: Amsterdam, 2009.

Esposito, Roberto. *Bìos: Biopolitics and Philosophy*. Translated by Timothy Campbell. Minneapolis: University of Minnesota Press, 2008. First published in Italian in 2004.

Foucault, Michel. *Dits et Écrits*. 4 vols. Paris: Gallimard, 1994.

Gatens, Moira. *Imaginary Bodies: Ethics, Power, and Corporeality*. London: Routledge, 1995.

Göhler, Gerhard, Kurt Lenk, Herfried Münkler, and Manfred Walther, eds. *Politische Institutionen im gesellschaftlichen Umbruch: Ideengeschichtliche Beiträge zur Theorie politischer Institutionen*. Opladen: Westdeutscher Verlag, 1990.

Hardt, Michael, and Antonio Negri. *Commonwealth*. Cambridge, Mass.: Harvard University Press, 2009.

——. *Multitude: War and Democracy in the Age of Empire*. New York: Penguin, 2004.

Heidegger, Martin. *Sein und Zeit* (1927). English translation: *Being and Time*. Translated by Joan Stambaugh. Albany: SUNY Press, 1996.

Illuminati, Augusto. "Sul principio di obbligazione." In Morfino and Piro, *Spinoza, resistenza e conflitto.*

Israel, Jonathan I. *Radical Enlightenment: Philosophy and the Making of Modernity, 1650–1750.* New York: Oxford University Press, 2001.

Jacob, Margaret C. *The Radical Enlightenment: Pantheists, Freemasons and Republicans.* London-Boston: Allen and Unwin, 1981; second edition: Morristown: The Temple Publishers, 2003.

Jacquet, Chantal. *Les Expressions de la puissance d'agir chez Spinoza.* Paris: Presses de la Sorbonne, 2005.

——. *Sub specie aeternitatis: Étude des concepts de temps, durée et éternité chez Spinoza.* Paris: Kimé, 1997.

Lilti, Antoine. "Comment écrit-on l'histoire intellectuelle des Lumières? Spinozisme, radicalisme et philosophie." In *Annales HSS* (64th year, no. 1), 2009, pp. 171–206.

Macpherson, Crawford Brough. *The Political Theory of Possessive Individualism: Hobbes to Locke.* Oxford: Oxford University Press, 1962.

Matheron, Alexandre. *Le Christ et le salut des Ignorants chez Spinoza.* Paris: Éditions Aubier-Montaigne, 1971.

——. *Individu et communauté chez Spinoza.* Paris: Minuit, 1969.

Merleau-Ponty, Maurice. *Signes.* Paris: Gallimard, 1960. English translation: *Signs.* Translated by Richard McCleary. Evanston, Ill.: Northwestern University Press, 1964.

Moreau, Pierre-François. *Spinoza: L'expérience et l'éternité.* Paris: PUF, 1994.

Morfino, V., and F. Piro, eds. *Spinoza, resistenza e conflitto*, in *Quaderni materialisti* no. 5. Milan: Ghibli, 2006.

Nairn, Tom. "Make for the Boondocks." *London Review of Books*, 5 May 2005.

Negri, Antonio. *L'Anomalie sauvage: Puissance et pouvoir chez Spinoza.* Translated by F. Matheron. Paris: PUF, 1982; republished Paris: Editions Amsterdam, 2006. English translation: *The Savage Anomaly: The Power of Spinoza's Metaphysics and Politics.* Translated by Michael Hardt. Minneapolis: University of Minnesota Press, 1991. The Italian original was published in 1981.

——. *Descartes politico o della ragionevole ideologia.* Milan: Feltrinelli, 1970; reprinted Rome: Manifestolibri, 2007. English translation: *Political Descartes: Reason, Ideology, and the Bourgeois Project.* Translated by Matteo Mandarini and Alberto Toscano. London: Verso, 2007.

———. "Giorgio Agamben: The Discreet Taste of the Dialectic." In *Giorgio Agamben: Sovereignty and Life*, edited by Matthew Calarco and Steven DeCaroli. Stanford: Stanford University Press, 2007.

———. *Kairòs, Alma Venus, multitude*. Translated by Judith Revel. Paris: Calmann-Lévy, 2001.

———. "Note sulla storia del politico in Tronti." In *L'Anomalia selvaggia*, appendix 3, pp. 288–292. Milan: Feltrinelli, 1981.

———. *Spinoza subversif: Variations (in)actuelles*. Translated by M. Raiola and F. Matheron. Paris: Kimé, 1994. English translation: *Subversive Spinoza: (Un)contemporary Variations*. Edited by Timothy S. Murphy. Translated by Timothy S. Murphy, Michael Hardt, Ted Stolze, and Charles T. Wolfe. Manchester: Manchester University Press, 2004.

Nietzsche, Friedrich. *Beyond Good and Evil*. In *Basic Writings of Nietzsche*, translated by Walter Kaufmann. New York: Modern Library, 1968.

———. *The Gay Science*. Translated by Walter Kaufmann. New York: Vintage, 1974.

Rancière, Jacques. *Disagreement: Politics and Philosophy*. Translated by Julie Rose. Minneapolis: University of Minnesota Press, 1999. The French original was published in 1995.

Rawls, John. *Lectures on the History of Political Philosophy*. Cambridge, Mass.: Harvard University Press, 2007.

Secrétan, Catherine, Tristan Dagron, and Laurent Bove, eds. *Qu'est-ce que les Lumières "radicales"?* Paris: Amsterdam, 2007.

Senn, Marcel, and Manfred Walther, eds. *Ethik, Recht, und Politik bei Spinoza*. Zurich: Schulthess, 2001.

Severino, Emanuele. "Spinoza, Dio, e il Nulla." *Corriere della Sera*, 30 June 2007.

Spinoza, Baruch. *Ethics*. In *Opera/Werke*, edited and translated by Konrad Blumenstock, vol. 2. Darmstadt: Wissenschaftliche Buchgesellschaft, 1967.

———. *Tractatus theologico-politicus*. Translated by Samuel Shirley. Leiden: Brill, 1991.

Virno, Paolo. "Il cosìdetto 'male' e la critica dello Stato." *Forme di vita* 4 (2005): 9–36.

Walther, Manfred. "Institution, Imagination, und Freiheit bei Spinoza: Eine kritische Theorie politischer Institutionen." In Göhler et al., *Politische Institutionen im gesellschaftlichen Umbruch*, pp. 246–275.

Zourabichvili, François. "L'enigma della 'moltitudine libera.'" In Morfino and Piro, *Spinoza, resistenza e conflitto*, p. 108.

INDEX

amor (*continued*)
and mystical overtones of term, 97; in sociology of Spinoza, xvi–xvii, 97–98; toward God, 61–62, 89–92; and unfolding of *potentia*, 2, 8, 25–26, 51, 61, 79, 88, 94, 97

appetitus: *vs.* Heideggerian *Besorgen*, 60; and imagination, origin of, 8, 51; and unfolding of *potentia*, 94

The Archeology of Knowledge (Foucault), 96

Aristotelianism, 19

Autonomia movement, x

Badiou, Alain, xiv, 21–22, 24

Balibar, Étienne, xi, 29–30, 81, 92

being: condition of by institutions and history, 5; dialectic of modernist philosophy and, 55–58; Heidegger on, 56–60, 63, 64, 67–68; Spinoza on, 39, 60–62, 63, 64

Being and Time (Heidegger), 57

being-multitude form of multitude-singularity relationship, 73–75

Beyond Good and Evil (Nietzsche), 71

biopolitics: biopolitical consciousness of Spinoza, 63, 98; and *cupiditates*, action of, 93–94; definition of, 93; *potentia* and *potestas* in context of, 25, 28, 46, 63

Bios: linking of being to, 63; proletariat movement defined in terms of, 46–47

Bodin, Jean: and political theology, 32; and sovereignty, theory of, 37, 38; and transcendent vision, xiv

Bourdieu, Pierre, xvii, 83, 93

Bove, Laurent, 8, 17, 96

Briefings on Existence (Badiou), 22

capitalism: and *cupiditates*, resistance to power by, 93; failure of, 3; ideology of modernity as justification of, 35–38; and modern alienation, 6; necessity of dismantling, xviii–xix; postmodern phase of, and immanentism of Spinoza, 20; Spinoza's conception of alternatives to, viii; subsumption of society under, and Western materialism, 28; and suppression of true democracy, viii

Certeau, Michel de, 96

Le Christ et le salut des Ignorants chez Spinoza (Matheron), 29

citizens' alienation, as inevitable consequence of sovereign state, 38

citizens' potency: revealing of, as first goal of revolution, 45–46, 51; rise of concept, 39–40; stripping recognition of from citizens, 37–38; transfer of to sovereign, 37. See also *potentia*

collective action, and reinvention of history, 45–46

the common: attraction toward, through imagination, 8, 51; characteristics of, 49–51; as common against public, 50; dynamic interplay with singularities, surplus created in, 53; as ever-open process of construction, 50; expropriation of by sovereign, 37–38; intuitive knowledge of through praxis, 78–79; as surplus, 50–51. *See also* the multitude

the common, production of: *cupiditas* and, 98; heresy as opening to, 44; joy inherent in, 82–83; multitude's propensity toward, as issue, 29–31; as only alternative to capitalism, 31; political realism and, 32–33; through *potentia*, 26. See also *potentia*, unfolding of from *conatus* to *amor*

common action, potency of: revealing of, as first goal of revolution, 45–46, 51; stripping recognition of from citizens, 37–38; transfer of to sovereign, 37. See also *potentia*

common reality, reappropriation of, immanence in revolution and, 48–49

Commonwealth (Negri and Hardt), xiii, xiv, 25

communism: and democracy, Negri's fusion of, ix; elaboration of Spinoza's *conatus* in, 40; reactionary responses to, and terrain of immanence, 41–43. *See also* revolution

conatus: binding of to *cupiditas*, 80–81; as effort to exist, 85; and emotions, effect of, 85; Foucault's production of subjectivity and, 28; *vs.* Heideggerian *Anwesenheit*, 60; and imagination, origin of, 8, 51; within individualistic framework, 86–87; as internal to potency of multitude, 12; Marxism as elaboration of, 404; as never-failing potency, 87; origin of liberty in, 12–13; origin of political institutions in, 12–13, 38; sociological discipline on, 84; and sociology of Spinoza, xvi–xvii, 85, 88, 94; and unfolding of *potentia*, 2, 8, 25–26, 51, 85, 88, 94

Conflict of the Faculties (Kant), 41

crisis, political and economic, as impetus for Spinoza's political turn, xii–xiii

cupiditas: and *amor*, critics' misunderstanding of relationship between, 52; binding of to *conatus*, 80–81; and emotions, effect of, 89; grounding of ethics in, as inconsistent with principles of modernity, 17–18; *vs.* Heideggerian *Entschlossenheit*, 60; ideologies of inevitable defeat of, 42–43; and imagination, 51; individualist interpretations of Spinoza and, 9; multitude as, 50; nature of, 88, 89; as never-excessive, 66; and production of the common, 98; resistance to power by, 93; and singularities' desire for multitude, 5, 15, 74, 75;

Empire (Negri and Hardt), xiii, xiv, 25
Enlightenment: Kant as man of, 41; materialism of, *vs.* materialism of Spinoza, 18–20; Spinoza as foundation of, 17
Epicurus, and materialist immanentism, 19
Esposito, Roberto, 102n38
essence and existence, dialectic of in modern philosophy, 55–58
eternity, Spinoza on, 61–62
ethical ontology of Spinoza, xv
Ethics (Spinoza): analogies to work of Foucault, 96; and construction of the common, 78; and definition of singularities, 71–73; on emotions, 85–86, 88–89; formulation of *summa potestas* in, 6; and genealogy of productive social desire, xvi; identity of presence and eternity in, 61; on love of God, 61–62, 89–92; ontology and anthropology of creative relations in, vii; *potestas vs. potentia* in, xii; on rapport between singularity and multitude, 76; as source of Spinoza's political thought, 9, 52
ethics, grounding of in desire, as inconsistent with principles of modernity, 17–18
exchange value, freedom from, reappropriation of common reality and, 49
existence, in modern philosophy, 55–58

Fabiani, Jean-Louis, 96–97
financial world, reappropriation of, 48–49
Foucault, Michel: and biopolitics, 25, 28; and the common, possibility of creating, 33; critiques of, 25; and escape from grasp of capitalism, 28; and French subversive tradition, 44; on history, conflictual character of, 11–12; and immanence terrain of social analysis, xvii; Negri on, xi; on production of subjectivity, 28; and sociology of Spinoza, xvi–xvii, 95–97
Frankfurt school, 27–28, 102n38
freedom. *See* liberty
French philosophy, subversive strain in, 44–46

The Gay Science (Nietzsche), 70–71
German philosophy, and essence and existence, separation of, 55–58
God: as cause and substance of all existence, 71–73, 78; human mind as part of, 23, 61, 62; knowledge of through praxis *vs.* theory, 78; love of, 61–62, 89–92; as *potentia*, 40, 53; in Spinoza, Severino on, 22–23
God, or Nature (*Deus, sive Natura*; Spinoza), ix
Goffman, Irving, 83
government, legitimate, Spinoza on, 38, 40

government by the multitude: and abuse of power, 76–78, 81; as inconsistent with principles of modernity, 17–18; process of establishing, 75–78; and unfolding of *potentia* as *amor*, 77–78; vices of multitude and, 77

Gramsci, Antonio, 5, 29–30, 31

Guattari, Félix: on the common, possibility of creating, 33; and escape from grasp of capitalism, 28; and French subversive tradition, 44; Negri on, xi; and use value, search for, 47–48

Guéroult, Martial, 26

Hardt, Michael, xiii, xiv, 25

Hegel, Georg Wilhelm Friedrich: concept of acosmism in, 52–53; and immanence, preoccupation with, 41; and philosophy of modernity, 18, 55–56, 58; on Spinoza, 23, 63–64; synthesis of public and sovereign in, 38; and transcendent vision, xv; and triumph of modern state, 56

Hegel or Spinoza (Macherey), xv

Heidegger, Martin: on being (*Da-Sein*), 56–60, 63, 64, 67–68; on being as *mit-Sein*, 63, 64, 68; and being-for-death, 14, 58, 66; commonalities with Spinoza, 62–63; on destiny, 57, 58, 65, 68; and existential temporality, xv–xvi; Illuminati on, 14; on liberty, 66; on Nietzsche, reactionary strain in, 66–67; on

potent immanence, possibility of, 57–60; as reactionary and fascist, 6, 64, 68; and rupture of modernity, 62–63; and socialism, 5; Spinoza as reversal of, 60, 63–68; Spinozan presence as fulfillment of potential in, 60; Spinoza's bifurcation of modern philosophy and, 27; and subsumption of society under capitalism, 65; and transcendence, xv–xvi, 5, 42; and Western materialism, 28

heresy: and opening to construction of the common, 44; as refusal of transcendence, 43–44; of Spinoza, 10, 53; tradition of underlying modern philosophy, 38–40, 44–49. *See also* sedition

history: conflictual character of, 11–12; in Heidegger, 57

history of ideas approach to Spinoza's philosophy, 16–21

Hobbes, Thomas: and modernity, philosophy of, 18; and sovereignty, modern theory of, 37, 38; and static definition of *conatus*, 86–87; and transcendent vision, xiv

Husserl, Edmund, 63, 64, 67

Illuminati, Augusto, 14

imagination: and attraction toward common, 8, 51; and institutions, construction of, 51; Moses's constitution as act of, 47; origin of in Spinoza, 8, 51; as potency on edge of rationality, 51; Spinoza's immanence as act of, 46–47

immanence: appropriation of concept by reactionary responses to Spinoza, 41–43; Heidegger on possibility of, 57–60

immanence in Spinoza, xiv–xv; as act of imagination, 46–47; advantages over classical and modern materialism, 18–20, 80–82; and caesura of Marxism, 20; as constitutive, 8–9; and liberation from dialecticism, 20, 29; movement of Spinoza's philosophy to, xii–xiii; nature of, 38–39; philosophy based on, characteristics of, 45–46, 48–49; as productive of the polis, 38; and revolution, 45–46, 48–49; unfolding of *potentia* and, 51. *See also* materialism of Spinoza

impotency, modern ideologies of, 42–43

individualism: and *conatus*, 86–87; as foreign to Spinoza, 18; interpretations of Spinoza, critique of, 4–5, 6–11; and sociology, 86–87

Individu et communauté (Matheron), 28

interrelationism, and processes of resistance, 95

Israel, Jonathan, xii, 16–17

Italian Communist Party (PCI), Negri and, x–xi

ius and *potentia*, tendential unity of in Spinoza, 7

Jacob, Margaret Candee, 16–17

Jacquet, Chantal, 29

kairòs, democratic action and, viii

Kant, Immanuel: Heidegger's reformulation of, 56–57; as man of the Enlightenment, 41; on reactionary responses to liberty, 41; on terrorism of oppressive theories, 42

katechon, as reintroduction of modernist political terms, 14, 15

knowledge, intuitive, through praxis in the common, 78–79

law: construction of through *making-multitude*, 75–77; and war, in modern political philosophy, 11–12. See also *potestas*

Lenin, Vladimir, xi

liberty: defense of, as telos of political activity in Spinoza, 7–8, 76; Heidegger on, 66; as invention of cooperation, in Spinoza, 42; origin of in *conatus*, 8, 12–13, 66; as potency constructing the common, 10, 15, 19; as product of desire, 65; Spinoza on, 53, 62; struggle for, and creation of new subjectivities, 33

Lilti, Antoine, 17

love. See *amor*

Lucretius, 19

Luxemburg, Rosa, xi

Macherey, Pierre, xi, xv, xvii, 92, 93

Machiavelli, Niccolò: elements of in Spinoza, 8; key terms of political thought in, 11; optimism about social transformation, 33; and political lineage of *seditio*, 11, 12, 13; and political struggle, familiarity with, ix–x; on Roman land redistribution, 49; and rupture of tradition of sovereignty, 39–40; Spinoza and, 5, 6

making-multitude form of multitude-singularity relationship, 75–77; and abuse of power, 76–78, 81; completion of, 78; and creation of political institutions, 75–78; joy inherent in, 82–83; obstacles to, 78–79; setbacks in, as insignificant, 79–80; as teleological, 77–78

Malebranche, Nicolas, 22

Marx, Karl: elaboration of Spinoza's *conatus* in, 40; on philosophy of modernity, 56

Marx Beyond Marx (Negri), ix

Marxism: reanimation of by postmodern reading of Spinoza, 5–6, 27; self-critique of 1960s and 70s, 20; on social relations of production *vs.* forces of production itself, xiv–xv

Marxists, attractiveness of Spinozism to, 46

materialism: classical and modern, advantages of Spinoza's materialism over, 18–20, 80–82; contemporary, and failure of real

socialism, 27; Western, failure of, 27–28

materialism of Spinoza: advantages over classical and modern materialism, 18–20, 80–82; as assertion of matter as productive force, 24; and construction of the common, 98; contemporary presentation of, 23–24, 29; and escape from capitalism, 29; and escape from dialecticism, 20, 29; *vs.* modernist materialism, 18–20. *See also* immanence in Spinoza

Matheron, Alexandre: as notable Spinoza scholar, 3; and possibility of escape from capitalism, 28–29; on Spinoza, 26–27; and Spinoza renaissance, xi, 92

matter in Spinoza: as productive force, 23–24; theological readings of, 21–22

Mens, vs. Heideggerian *Umsicht*, 60

Merleau-Ponty, Maurice, 45–46

Mészáros, István, 44

metaphysics, 17th-century politicization of, 37

mind, power over emotions, 90–92

mit-Sein: being as, in Heidegger and Spinoza, 63, 64, 68; as continuous opening, 63

modernity, philosophy of: bifurcation of after Spinoza, 26–27; and definition of being, 56–58; dialectic unity of essence and existence in, 55–58; heretical tradition underlying, 38–40,

44–49; individualism and sovereign power as basis of, 18; as justification of capitalist relations of production, 35–38; key terms of political thought in, 11; materialism of, *vs.* materialism of Spinoza, 18–20, 80–82; potency in, 55–56; reintroduction of political terms of, 13–14; Spinoza's philosophy as inconsistent with, 15–16, 16–21

Moreau, Pierre-François, xi, 92

Moro, Aldo, xi

Multitude (Negri and Hardt), xiii, xiv, 25

the multitude: and autonomy of the political, 14–15; collective action by, and reinvention of history, 45–46; as *cupiditas*, 50; gravitation of individuals toward, 15; irreducibility of to "the people," 77; propensity toward production of the common, as issue, 29–31; reality of, 15; self-construction of, 15; Spinoza on barbarity of, 30; vices of, 77. *See also* the common

the multitude, formation of in *making-multitude*, 75–77; and abuse of power, 76–78, 81; completion of, 78; and creation of political institutions, 75–78; joy inherent in, 82–83; obstacles to, 78–79; setbacks in, as insignificant, 79–80; as teleological, 77–78

the multitude, government by: and abuse of power, 76–78, 81; as inconsistent with principles

of modernity, 17–18; process of establishing, 75–78; and unfolding of *potentia* as *amor*, 77–78; vices of multitude and, 77

the multitude, potency of: revealing of, as first goal of revolution, 45–46, 51; rise of concept, 39–40; stripping recognition of from citizens, 37–38; transfer of to sovereign, 37. *See also potentia*

the multitude, rapport between singularities and: completion of, 78; as core of Spinozism of 1968, 69–70, 71, 81–82; critics' denial of, 69–70, 81–82; desire for multitude as basis of, 74; as essential characteristic of singularities, 73; in *making-multitude* mode, 75–77; mutation of singularities into civil beings, xvi, 73, 74; as teleological, 77–78. *See also making-multitude* form of multitude-singularity relationship

the multitude-singularity relationship: *being-multitude* form of, 73–75; *making-multitude* form of, 75–77. *See also* multitude, rapport between singularities and

mutation of singularities, moment of, xvi, 73, 74

Nairn, Tom, 81

natural law tradition: individualistic dimension, elimination of through *conatus*, 94; and sociology of Spinoza, 84; and transcendent view, xvii

Negri, Antonio: critics of, xi, 1, 2; on democracy, meaning of, viii–ix; erudition of, x; fusing of theory and praxis by, ix; inscription of philosophical into contemporary political by, ix–x, xiii, xvii; later career of, xiii; as political activist, ix–xi; political asylum in France, xi; political struggle, nature of, x–xi; prison sentence of, xi; and revolutionary praxis, new image of, xi; on Spinoza's central insight, viii; on Spinoza's turn from transcendence, xii–xiii; style of analysis of, ix–x, xvii, xviii

neoliberalism: concept of democracy, *vs.* Spinoza, vii; failure of, 3

Nicolas-Le Strat, Pascal, 96

Nietzsche, Friedrich: on choice between love of life and death, 65, 66; denial of *potentia* in Spinoza's philosophy, 70–71, 80; on philosophy of modernity, 56; on Spinoza as idealist, xvi; Spinoza's influence on, 70; on theological readings of Spinoza, 21–22; on will to power, teleology of nature and, 71, 80

Nizan, Paul, 46

normative theory, sociology of Spinoza as, 84

ontological space, as plenum, in Spinoza, 62, 82

ontology of actuality: and common, construction of, 50; and production of subjectivity, 20, 48, 50

pain, Spinoza on, 85–86, 88–89

pantheism of Spinoza, 98

PCI. *See* Italian Communist Party

phenomenological being, in Heidegger *vs.* Spinoza, 64–66

phenomenologists, and *epistémè* of communism for tomorrow, 3

philosophy of 20th century: polarity of Heidegger and Spinoza and, 67–68; polarity of Husserl and Wittgenstein and, 64

philosophy of modernity: bifurcation of after Spinoza, 26–27; and definition of being, 56–58; dialectic unity of essence and existence in, 55–58; heretical tradition underlying, 38–40, 44–49; individualism and sovereign power as basis of, 18; as justification of capitalist relations of production, 35–38; key terms of political thought in, 11; materialism of, *vs.* materialism of Spinoza, 18–20; potency in, 55–56; reintroduction of political terms of, 13–14; Spinoza's philosophy as inconsistent with, 15–16, 16–21

pleasure, Spinoza on, 85–86, 88–89

the political: as dynamic between singularities and common, 53; individualist interpreters of Spinoza on, 9–10; as source and active property of social structure, 52; as source and rupture of the social, 10; as sovereignty, continual reemergence of concept, 29–30

the political, autonomy of: free
multitude and, 14–15; meaning
of, 14; origin of concept, 12; and
seditio, 12
political action, philosophy and, 3.
See also revolution
Political Descartes (Negri), ix
political institutions: individualist
interpreters of Spinoza on, 6–7;
production of self and, 98
political institutions, formation
of: and abuse of power, 76–78,
81; through *conatus*, 12–13, 38;
through desire for free multitude, 5, 15; through *making-multitude* process, 75–78
political philosophy, modern, law
and war in, 11–12
political realism, and the common,
possibility of, 32–33
political theology: *democratia
omnino absoluta* as, critics on,
31–32; nature of, 32
positivism: charges of against
Negri's reading of Spinoza, 26;
and recurrence of sovereignty
within politics, 30
postmodern age: relevance of
Spinoza's philosophy to, 4, 84,
92–93; Spinoza's consonance
with, 21; usage of Spinoza in,
4–6
poststructuralist philosophies,
impotence of, 28
potency: Heidegger on possibility of, 57–60; in philosophy of
modernity, 55–56

potentia: as always open, always
interrupted, 76; as central
concept in Spinoza, 4; *conatus* of
multitude as internal to, 12; construction of common through,
26; and emotions, effect of,
85; growth of with broadened
association, 7–8; *vs.* Heideggerian *Möglichkeit*, 60; and *ius*,
tendential unity of in Spinoza, 7;
and making of multitude, 75–76;
negative of, as non-existent,
10, 53; Nietzsche's failure to
recognize in Spinoza, 70–71, 80;
the political as, 10; and political
power, 13–16; singularities and,
80–81. *See also* citizens' potency
potentia, accumulation (surplus)
of: as action within and against
potestas, 25; the common as,
50–51; in dynamic interplay of
common with singularities, 53;
individualist interpreters of Spinoza on, 6–8; as monistic, 10
potentia, unfolding of from *conatus*
to *amor*: and creation of the
multitude, 79; critics of concept, 2; *cupiditas* and, 8, 51; and
government by the multitude,
77–78; and imagination, 8,
51; and sociology of Spinoza,
88, 94–95, 97–98; struggle of
potentia and *potestas* in, 25–26;
teleology of, 7–8
potentia vs. potestas, 13–16; as absolute antinomy, critics' claims of,
25; asymmetry between, 9, 26,

singularities: characteristics of, 73; as constructors of society, 40; definition of, 71–73; embedding of in eternity, 72–73; fear of solitude, as impetus to join the multitude, 73–74; mutation of into civil beings, xvi, 73, 74; potency of, 6–7, 80–81; productive relationality between, xvi; self-recognition and displacement in, 80–81

singularities, rapport between multitude and: completion of, 78; as core of Spinozism of 1968, 69–70, 71, 81–82; critics' denial of, 69–70, 81–82; desire for multitude as basis of, 74; as essential characteristic of singularities, 73; in *making-multitude* mode, 75–77; mutation of singularities into civil beings, xvi, 73, 74; as teleological, 77–78. See also *making-multitude* form of multitude-singularity relationship

situationism, 44

the social: as materially-based process, 8; the political as source and rupture of, 10; the political as transitive property of, 52. *See also* the multitude

social contract: Negri on, xv; Spinoza on, 75–76

socialism: ideological crisis of 1960s and 70s, 20; real, failure of, 3, 27

Socialism or Barbarism (Mészáros), 44

social process, material basis of in Spinoza, 8

sociology, as discipline: and Foucault, 96–97; individualist perspective on, 86–87, 94; major traditions in, 83–84; and naturalistic theories of the social, 84; and normative theory, 84; *vs.* sociology of Spinoza, 84–85, 87, 93

sociology of Spinoza: characteristics of, 84; construction of the common as goal of, 94–95, 97–98; as distinct from sociological discipline, 84–85, 87, 93; Foucault and, 95–97; love toward God and, 89–92; politics derived from, 98; and *potentia*, unfolding of from *conatus* to *amor*, 88, 94–95, 97–98

sovereignty: challenges to, by Descartes, 36; deconstruction of, and creation of the common, 50; determined by *potentia* of the multitude, 105n12; modern tradition of, exceptions and ruptures in, 38–40, 44–49; return of to citizens, in *making-multitude* mode, 76; 17th-century constructions of, necessity of transcendence concept in, 36–38; Spinoza on, 38, 40; transfer of citizens' power to, 37. *See also* the State

sovereignty, politics as: as continually-reemerging proposal, 29; *democratia omnino absoluta* as clean break from, 32

Soviet critical thought, and subversive tradition, 44

Spinoza, Baruch: as heretic, 10, 53; on Jubilee in Jewish history, 49; and Negri's discursive strategy, xvii; and neoliberalism, 3; political context of, Negri's attention to, xvii; and political lineage of *seditio*, 11, 12, 13, 15–16; political turn of, xii–xiii; and possibility of escape from capitalism, 28; and rupture of modernity, 62–63; 17th century views on, 4; on time, xv, 60–63

Spinoza for Our Time (Negri): new cooperative social and political subject defined in, xviii; overview of, xiii–xvii; roots of, ix; *The Subversive Spinoza* and, xiii

Spinoza renaissance: and bifurcation of modern philosophy, 27; critics of, 21–23, 24–26; and Marxist critique, reanimation of, 27; and rapport between singularities and multitude, 69–70, 71, 81–82

Spinoza's philosophy: antimodernism of, 84, 92–93; and *epistémè* of communism for tomorrow, 3; history of ideas approach to, 16–21; Marxism as elaboration of, 40; as method allowing simultaneous immanence and creative rupture, 46–47; modern rise of, 38; in postmodern context, 4–6; relevance to postmodern age, 4, 84, 92–93;

as reversal of Heidegger, 60, 63–68

Spinoza's political thought, *Ethics* and, 9, 52

spiritual ill-health, causes of, 91

Stalin, Josef, 32

the State: as barrier to democratic progress, 12; dialectic relationship with *conatus* of individual, 86–87; multitude's refusal of contract with, 7; as protector of capital accumulations, 36. *See also* political institutions; sovereignty

stateless society, *being-multitude* form of singularity-multitude rapport as, 73–75

structuralists, and *epistémè* of communism for tomorrow, 3

subjectivity, production of: and escape from capitalism, 30–31, 45–46; Foucault on, 28; immanence of, 4–5; ontology of actuality and, 20, 48, 50; and political institutions, creation of, 98; *potentia* and, 26

The Subversive Spinoza (Negri), xiii

surplus (accumulation) of *potentia*: as action within and against *potestas*, 25; the common as, 50–51; in dynamic interplay of common with singularities, 53; individualist interpreters of Spinoza on, 6–8; as monistic, 10

teleology: capitalist reformism as pretense of, 56; defense of liberty as telos of political activity in Spinoza, 7–8; immanentism of Spinoza as liberation from, 20; *making-multitude* as, 77–78; Nietzsche on, 80; in Spinoza, individualist interpreters of Spinoza on, 7

terrorism of oppressive theories, Kant on, 42

theological ideologies, individualist interpreters of Spinoza and, 7

Theological-Political Treatise (Spinoza): conception of democracy in, vii–viii; on constitution of singularities as multitude, 74; historicity of institutions in, 6; on Moses' act of imagination, 47; on *potentia*, growth of with broadened association, 7–8; and *potestas vs. potentia*, xii; on rapport between singularity and multitude, 76; and Spinoza's political turn, xii–xiii

theological readings of Spinoza, 21–22

Theory of the Subject (Badiou), 22

A Thousand Plateaus (Deleuze and Guattari), 33

time: Heidegger on, 57–61; Spinoza on, xv, 60–63

Tractatus theologico-politicus (Spinoza). See *Theological-Political Treatise* (Spinoza)

transcendence: abandonment by post-Marxian reactionary theory, 41–43; deconstruction of, and creation of the common, 50; Heidegger and, xv–xvi, 5, 42; new ethic of, 42; and 17th-century constructions of sovereignty, 36–38; Spinoza's turn from, xii–xiii, 5

use value: nostalgic view of, 48–49; search for, 47–48

virtue, Spinoza on: knowledge of God and, 78; as *potentia*, 78; transformation of nature into, 71, 92

vitalism, 64, 67

Walther, Manfred, 29–30

Weber, Max, 83

Wittgenstein, Ludwig, 64

world-creation, human, as the common of democracy, xvi

Zourabichvili, François, xii, 14–15

INSURRECTIONS: CRITICAL STUDIES IN RELIGION, POLITICS, AND CULTURE

Slavoj Žižek, Clayton Crockett, Creston Davis, Jeffrey W. Robbins, Editors